Corporate Director's Guidebook

FIFTH EDITION

Committee on Corporate Laws

ABA Section of
BUSINESS LAW

ABA

Defending Liberty
Pursuing Justice

Commitment to Quality: ABA Section of Business Law is committed to quality in our publications. Our authors are experienced practitioners in their fields. Prior to publication, the contents of all our books are rigorously reviewed by experts to ensure the highest quality product and presentation. Because we are committed to serving our readers' needs, we welcome your feedback on how we can improve future editions of this book.

The materials contained herein represent the opinions of the authors and editors and should not be construed to be the action of either the American Bar Association or the Section of Business Law unless adopted pursuant to the bylaws of the Association.

Nothing contained in this book is to be considered as the rendering of legal advice for specific cases, and readers are responsible for obtaining such advice from their own legal counsel. This book and any forms and agreements herein are intended for educational and informational purposes only.

Library of Congress Cataloging-in-Publication Data

Corporate director's guidebook / Committee on Corporate Laws. — 5th ed.
    p. cm.
  ISBN-13: 978-1-59031-850-8
  ISBN-10: 1-59031-850-1
    1. Directors of corporations—Legal status, laws, etc.—United States.
2. Corporation law—United States. I. American Bar Association. Committee on Corporate Laws.

KF1423.Z9C67 2007
346.73'066—dc22   2007026879

ISBN: 10: 1-59031-850-1
ISBN 13: 978-1-59031-850-8

10 09   5 4 3

Contents

Foreword

This is the fifth edition of the *Corporate Director's Guidebook*. Since its initial publication in 1978, the *Guidebook* has been relied upon by directors and business executives, as well as by those who advise them and by students of corporate governance. Indeed, the *Guidebook* has become the most frequently cited handbook in its field.

The primary purpose of the *Guidebook* is to provide concise guidance to corporate directors in meeting their responsibilities. The *Guidebook* focuses on the role of the individual director as well as the functions of the board of directors and its key committees. Although the *Guidebook's* organizing framework is based upon the law, we have made every effort to keep the prose free of legalisms because our target audience is corporate directors, not lawyers.

The fourth edition of the *Guidebook*, which was published in 2004, focused in large part on changes caused or influenced by the Sarbanes-Oxley Act, such as new standards of director independence, federally mandated responsibilities for the audit committee, and greatly expanded corporate governance standards for listed companies. This fifth edition assumes these as a baseline and urges boards of directors to rebalance their priorities to focus on business performance. If the importance of compliance with the law was the theme of the fourth edition, the theme of this fifth edition is the increasingly vital role that directors play in protecting investors' interests and in directing or overseeing corporate strategy and its execution by senior officers.

Specifically, this new, up-to-date edition of the *Guidebook* discusses, among many other developments, the following:

- Management and board advisors must take the lead in focusing on, and providing for, the conditions necessary for effective board understanding and involvement.
- Responsiveness—to shareholders, to regulators, and to the public—is increasingly the hallmark of an effective board. Although the board determines its own agenda, it should also be responsive to external forces.
- Being a director in today's environment requires an energetic and diligent dedication of purpose and a thorough understanding of the business, finances, and major transactions presented to the board.
- There are subtle but important changes in boardroom dynamics that have been facilitated by securities regulators because of their emphasis on a baseline level of legal and regulatory corporate compliance.
- Compensation decisions are subject to enhanced disclosure requirements and renewed shareholder and public interest.
- Many corporations have adopted a majority voting standard for director election in non-contested elections.

While the *Guidebook* provides important guidance to directors of public companies, it continues to have core relevance to all corporate directors in terms of their duties and obligations as well as boardroom best practices. The Committee on Corporate Laws encourages directors and their advisors to make ample use of this fifth edition of the *Guidebook*.

Respectfully submitted,

E. Norman Veasey, Chair

Herbert S. Wander, Chair-Designate

For the Committee
June 2007

Committee on Corporate Laws (2006–2007)

The Committee on Corporate Laws of the American Bar Association's Section of Business Law is composed of active or former practicing lawyers, law professors, regulators, and judges, with corporate expertise and from throughout the United States. In addition to the *Corporate Director's Guidebook* and other scholarly writings, the Committee is responsible for the development of the *Model Business Corporation Act*.

The *Model Act*, first issued in 1950, has been adopted substantially or largely in its entirety by more than 30 states in the United States and in important respects by many other states. The *Model Act* has played an important role in the development of corporate law in the United States and elsewhere.

The Committee serves as the permanent editorial board for the *Model Act*, reviewing, revising, and updating its provisions on a continuing basis. Moreover, the Committee publishes the *Model Business Corporation Act Annotated*, a comprehensive compilation of the *Model Act* and cases and authorities relevant to its provisions. The Fourth Edition is scheduled for release later in 2007.

The roster of active Committee participants during the development of the *Guidebook*'s fifth edition (including appointed members, consultants, and liaisons from other ABA committees) is listed below.

Stuart D. Ames
Miami, Florida

William H. Clark, Jr.
Philadelphia, Pennsylvania

James H. Cheek, III
Nashville, Tennessee

Thomas A. Cole
Chicago, Illinois

George W. Coleman
Dallas, Texas

Professor James D. Cox
Durham, North Carolina

Professor Michael P. Dooley,
Reporter
Charlottesville, Virginia

Professor Melvin A. Eisenberg
Berkeley, California

Professor Charles M. Elson
Newark, Delaware

Margaret M. Foran
New York, New York

Diane Holt Frankle
East Palo Alto, California

Mark J. Gentile
Wilmington, Delaware

Allen Cunningham Goolsby
Richmond, Virginia

Michael J. Halloran
Washington, DC

Professor Lawrence A. Hamermesh
Wilmington, Delaware

James J. Hanks, Jr.
Baltimore, Maryland

Carol Hansell
Toronto, Ontario

Professor Joseph Hinsey, IV
Boston, Massachusetts

The Honorable Jack B. Jacobs
Wilmington, Delaware

Michael L. Jamieson
Tampa, Florida

Mary Ann Jorgenson
Cleveland, Ohio

Stanley Keller
Boston, Massachusetts

Thomas J. Kim
Washington, DC

James I. Lotstein
Hartford, Connecticut

Professor Lisabeth A. Moody
St. Petersburg, Florida

D. Craig Nordlund
Santa Clara, California

Trevor S. Norwitz
New York, New York

Robert L. Nutt
Boston, Massachusetts

John F. Olson
Washington, DC

Kim K.W. Rucker
Dallas, Texas

Overview

For over a century, the corporation has been the principal form of business enterprise in the United States. A primary purpose of the corporate form is to enable investors to participate financially in a business enterprise, while at the same time limiting their financial exposure to the amount of their investment. Because shareholders do not have the right to manage the corporation, the board of directors' oversight and direction of the management of the business and affairs of the corporation are fundamental to the protection of shareholders' interests and to the effective performance of the corporation.

Although the appropriate allocation of authority among the shareholders, the board of directors, and management can be debated, it is difficult to imagine any system of effective governance of a significant, publicly owned business enterprise without an intermediary between the owners and the managers, such as a board of directors, with the time, resources, information, and experience to direct strategies and oversee the managers and operations of the business. State corporation law supports and strengthens this system by imposing legal duties on directors.

This *Guidebook* is geared to the individual director and provides guidance to directors of business corporations, who are elected by the shareholders of the corporation and have a duty to advance the interests of the corporation to the exclusion of their own interests. Accountable to the corporation's shareholders, a director is nonetheless required to exercise independent judgment and is not merely an agent of the corporation's shareholders. Directors have to make decisions applying their business judgment based on reasonably available information and have to act in what they reasonably believe to be the best interests of the corporation. In some cases, a board may even make a decision, in good faith, knowing that a substantial percentage of shareholders might disagree with that decision.

This *Guidebook* aims to help directors be effective in fulfilling their duties to the corporation. Although the emphasis is on directors of a public company—a corporation with public shareholders and a trading market for its securities—the *Guidebook* has relevance for every corporate director. It explains the applicable legal standards of director conduct, summarizes a director's functions and responsibilities, and addresses the operations and practices of the board of directors and its committees, with particular focus on the customary independent committees of a public corporation board—the audit, compensation, and nominating/corporate governance committees.

Although directors are responsible for overseeing and directing the operation of the business and affairs of the corporation, most directors are not managers. A key challenge for outside directors is to oversee the corporation's activities effectively and make well-informed decisions without themselves usurping the role of management. This *Guidebook* helps directors meet that challenge by explaining how they can exercise their strategic and oversight responsibilities and by identifying the boardroom practices and procedures that support and promote effective director involvement. In addition, most directors are not lawyers. Directors serve themselves well by seeking legal advice to help them satisfy legal requirements and to support

A key challenge for outside directors is to oversee the corporation's activities effectively and make well-informed decisions without themselves usurping the role of management. This Guidebook helps directors meet that challenge by explaining how they can exercise their strategic and oversight responsibilities and by identifying the boardroom practices and procedures that support and promote effective director involvement.

(but not replace) the board's deliberative and decision-making processes.

Readers should bear in mind that directors can exercise their decision-making powers only by acting collectively, either as a board or as a board committee. Judgment, however, is exercised on an individual basis, and informed judgment depends upon individual preparation and participation as well as on group deliberation. Effective performance of the board's oversight function often results from an individual's recognition that a particular matter warrants inquiry or action.

The *Guidebook*'s description of director conduct is not intended as legal advice or a suggestion that different conduct will result in a violation of law or potential personal liability. Accordingly, readers should not infer any forecast of litigation or liability based upon failing to conform to the recommendations made in this *Guidebook*. Directors who perform their duties and responsibilities conscientiously will decrease their risk of liability for deficient performance.

Each corporation is a creature of the corporation statute of its state of incorporation, and the states' corporation laws differ in various respects. The same is true with respect to judicial decisions of the various state courts explicating the legal duties of directors. The guidance contained in this *Guidebook* is generally applicable to all business corporations, regardless of their state of incorporation. The *Guidebook* also addresses the federal securities laws and regulations as they relate to boards of directors and the major securities markets' listing standards that mandate specific governance practices. Corporations are also subject to other legal requirements that can affect corporate governance, such as the regulatory regimes applicable to financial institutions, public utilities, investment companies, and other business enterprises licensed or regulated at the federal or state level. This *Guidebook* does not address industry-specific regulations.

Joining a Board of Directors

Joining a board and serving as a director can and should be a challenging, exciting, and rewarding experience. It also requires a significant personal investment of time and attention. By joining a board, an individual puts his or her reputation at stake with that of the company and the other board members. Moreover, by joining a board, an individual must fulfill a director's legal duties of care and loyalty. Consequently, the decision whether to join a board should not be made casually. An individual considering an invitation to join a board should carefully

> *An individual considering an invitation to join a board should carefully study the corporation, its business, its history, its board, and its senior management and should understand the reasons for the invitation and the board's expectations.*

study the corporation, its business, its history, its board, and its senior management and should understand the reasons for the invitation and the board's expectations. For example, would the candidate be expected to serve in any particular role on the board or any of its committees—perhaps as the lead director or as a designated "financial expert" on the audit committee?

This discussion is tailored for the public company director. Most directors of private corporations will have some ownership interest in or connection to the corporation or its owners. If asked to join the board of a private company or a closely controlled company, an individual should explore what role is intended for an outsider on the board; understand the corporation's shareholder base (including any factions among the shareholders) and the directors' relationships with the shareholders; determine whether independent legal advice will be available if requested (and, if so, from whom); inquire whether an initial public offering of the corporation is contemplated; and consider taking some of the steps described in the following list, such as reviewing the corporation's financial information and becoming familiar with its director and officer insurance coverage.

When asked to join the board of a public company, an individual should first consider these basic questions:

- whether the opportunity to serve on the board is sufficiently compelling to engage the individual's serious interest and attention in light of any competing commitments;
- whether the individual has (i) sufficient time and flexibility to perform diligently the required duties for a director of that company, especially if a corporate crisis or major transaction should arise; (ii) scheduling conflicts that would unduly interfere with the board's normal meeting schedule; (iii) the requisite skills and experience to participate meaningfully as a director of that company; and (iv) any present, foreseeable, or perceived conflicts of interest with the corporation, its business, or its senior management (e.g., material relationships with competitors, potential acquisition targets, or potential acquirers);
- whether the individual has or can develop a sufficient depth of understanding of the corporation's business and business model to be an effective director; and
- whether the individual believes that senior management and the board have integrity and conduct themselves in an honest and ethical manner.

If the director candidate is still interested in the opportunity and believes that he or she has the ability to be an effective director and add value to the corporation, then the following steps should be taken:

- meet with the nominating/corporate governance committee chair or other board representative who extended the invitation, and with the chief executive officer (CEO) and perhaps other senior members of management, to discuss the principal issues facing the corporation, board organization and procedures, and the committee memberships contemplated for the individual;

- assess the attitude of the CEO and senior management toward board activity—whether a proactive board and independent director judgment are truly desired;
- learn about the corporation, including the nature of its business, its financial condition, and stability of its current business activities and future prospects, by reviewing the corporation's recent public disclosure documents, such as press releases, investor presentations, and SEC filings;
- determine whether there are company-specific factors requiring special attention—for example, a financially challenged or distressed corporation may require specialized experience or a greater than usual time commitment; and
- gather information about the corporation's reputation in the investment community and in the business world generally, by reviewing press and analyst reports and conducting Internet and other searches.

If, following this preliminary diligence, the candidate understands the corporation's business activities, as well as its risks and prospects, and has a continuing and serious interest in the directorship opportunity, the following additional steps should be considered:

- learn the structure and processes the board uses to provide effective oversight, including (i) the corporation's corporate governance principles or guidelines and committee charters, (ii) the routine operation of the board and its committees, (iii) the methods employed for monitoring and evaluating board and committee performance, and (iv) the procedures for senior executive officer appointments, evaluation, and succession planning;
- review the audit committee's membership and procedures and meet with the audit committee chair to discuss any recent or current critical financial or accounting issues

(including rating agency concerns, if any), the clarity and transparency of public disclosures respecting the corporation's financial affairs, and the effectiveness of the corporation's programs to address legal compliance issues and risks;

- review recent examples of the "meeting book" provided to directors in advance of meetings and other information regularly provided to the directors;
- identify the corporation's regular internal and external legal and financial advisors and learn their role and participation in the corporation's and the board's activities;
- understand, based on appropriate professional advice, the corporation's director exculpation, indemnification, and litigation expense advancement provisions in organizational documents and contracts, the amount and coverage provided by the corporation's directors' and officers' liability insurance, the quality of the corporation's insurance carrier(s), and whether the corporation has provided the outside directors with separate insurance;
- receive a briefing on significant claims or litigation against the corporation, especially any that involve the activities of the board of directors or involve any entity with which the prospective director is already affiliated; and
- understand director compensation arrangements and determine whether they are commensurate with the effort required and the risk undertaken.

Reimbursement by the corporation of reasonable out-of-pocket expenses, such as travel expenses, incurred by the candidate in conducting this due diligence would typically be appropriate. The corporation may also require a confidentiality commitment from the candidate covering nonpublic information regarding the corporation's business and affairs disclosed to the candidate.

In addition to the diligence steps outlined above, a candidate should attempt to assess the board's culture to the extent feasible from his or her perspective. When serving on a board, directors often value most the opportunity to collaborate on tough issues with other experienced business people who bring a wide variety of approaches, styles, and experience to boardroom deliberations. This puts a premium on each director's ability to work toward building a consensus. To facilitate this collaboration and decision-making process, directors must be able to formulate and articulate their views and to engage in constructive dialogue in an atmosphere of mutual respect and confidentiality.

When serving on a board, directors often value most the opportunity to collaborate on tough issues with other experienced business people who bring a wide variety of approaches, styles, and experience to boardroom deliberations. To facilitate collaboration and the decision-making process, directors must be able to formulate and articulate their views and to engage in constructive dialogue in an atmosphere of mutual respect and confidentiality.

Responsibilities, Rights, and Duties of a Corporate Director

A business corporation's core objective is to create and increase wealth for its shareholders. Directors provide leadership toward this objective through two primary functions: decision making and oversight. The directors' decision-making function generally involves considering and, if warranted, approving corporate policy and strategic goals and taking specific actions such as evaluating and selecting top management, approving major expenditures, and acquiring and disposing of material assets. The directors' oversight function involves monitoring the corporation's business and affairs including, for example, financial performance, management performance, and compliance with legal obligations and corporate policies.

In performing their decision-making and oversight functions, directors have, individually or collectively, various responsibilities and rights. Corporate governance standards created in recent years by the Sarbanes-Oxley Act, Securities and Exchange Commission (SEC) rulemaking, and securities market regulations, as well as judicial interpretations of state laws, have increased the compliance and disclosure requirements for the board and management of public companies, but they do not change the fundamental principles governing director action or duties.

A. Overall Responsibilities

The relationship between the board and management of the corporation is set forth in state corporation statutes. In general, state laws provide that all corporate powers shall be exercised by or under the authority of the board of directors of the corporation, and its business and affairs shall be managed by or under the direction of, and subject to the oversight of, the board.

State corporate statutes emphasize the board's responsibility to oversee the management of the corporation. Although these statutes do not specifically define this responsibility, it generally includes the following tasks for the board and its committees:

- monitoring the corporation's performance in light of its operating, financial, and other significant corporate plans, strategies, and objectives, and approving major changes in plans and strategies;
- selecting the CEO, setting the goals for the CEO and other senior executives, evaluating and establishing their compensation, and making changes when appropriate;
- developing, approving, and implementing succession plans for the CEO and top senior executives;
- understanding the corporation's risk profile and reviewing and overseeing risk management programs;
- understanding the corporation's financial statements and monitoring the adequacy of its financial and other internal controls as well as its disclosure controls and procedures; and
- establishing and monitoring effective compliance systems and policies for ethical conduct.

The board is the guardian of the corporation's integrity. The board encourages senior management to establish the proper "tone at the top" by setting clear expectations for the corporation's ethical behavior and conduct of its business in compliance with law.

The board is the guardian of the corporation's integrity. The board encourages senior management to establish the proper "tone at the top" by setting clear expectations for the corporation's ethical behavior and conduct of its business in compliance with law. While the CEO and senior management must take the leadership role to promote integrity, honesty, and ethical conduct throughout the organization, the board should monitor management's operating style and support and encourage these values.

1. Board Responsibilities

The board's principal responsibilities are to select the top management for the corporation, plan for succession, and provide general direction and guidance with respect to the corporation's strategy and management's conduct of the business. In so doing, the board should give significant consideration to the corporation's financial and business objectives. At the same time, the board must oversee that the corporation is conducting its affairs in accordance with law.

A number of state corporation statutes expressly allow the board to consider the interests of employees, suppliers, and customers, as well as the communities in which the corporation operates and the environment. Although the board may consider the interests of these other constituencies, the board is accountable primarily to shareholders for the performance of the corporation. Non-shareholder constituency considerations are best understood not as independent corporate objectives but as factors to be taken into account in pursuing the best interests of the corporation. Being responsive to stakeholder interests and concerns can help to contribute positively to a corporation's workplace culture as well as its reputation for integrity and ethical behavior.

Being responsive to stakeholder interests and concerns can help to contribute positively to a corporation's workplace culture as well as its reputation for integrity and ethical behavior.

Each director works for the benefit of the corporation and all of its owners. This is true even if a director is nominated or designated by a subset of the shareholder body (e.g., holders of preferred stock who may have special rights to elect a director), elected in a proxy contest, or appointed by the board to fill a vacancy.

2. *Individual Responsibilities*

To be effective in decision-making and oversight activities, a director must understand the corporation's operations, including its areas of business and the competitive environment in which it operates. This knowledge enables the director to evaluate independently corporate and senior management performance, to provide strategic guidance, to work with management and other directors in developing and evaluating corporate objectives and strategic plans, and to challenge, support, and compensate management as warranted. Accordingly, the director's understanding of the corporation and its industry should include:

- the corporation's business activities;
- the key drivers underlying the corporation's profitability and cash flow—how the corporation makes money—as a whole and also in its significant business segments;
- the corporation's operational and financial plans, strategies, and objectives and how they further the goal of enhancing shareholder value;
- the corporation's economic, financial, regulatory, and competitive risks, as well as risks to the corporation's physical assets, intellectual property, and personnel;
- the corporation's financial condition and the results of its operations and of its significant business segments for recent periods; and
- the corporation's performance compared with that of its competitors.

In addition, a director should be satisfied that effective systems exist for timely reporting to, and consideration by, the board or relevant board committee of:

- corporate objectives and strategic plans;
- current business and financial performance of the corporation and its significant business segments, as compared to board-approved objectives and plans;
- systems of company controls designed to manage risk and to provide reasonable assurance of compliance with law and corporate policies; and

- material risk and liability contingencies, including industry risk, litigation, and regulatory matters.

Directors should do their homework. They should review board and committee meeting agendas and related materials sufficiently in advance of meetings to enable them to be well prepared and participate actively in the deliberative process. They should receive and review minutes of board meetings and keep informed about the activities of those board committees on which they do not serve. More generally, a director should have an attitude of constructive skepticism. Directors should not be reticent or passive. Indeed, to be a director means to direct—become informed, participate, ask questions, apply considered business judgment to matters brought before the board, and, when necessary, bring other matters to the full board's attention.

A director should have an attitude of constructive skepticism. Directors should not be reticent or passive. Indeed, to be a director means to direct—become informed, participate, ask questions, apply considered business judgment to matters brought before the board, and, when necessary, bring other matters to the full board's attention.

B. Rights

Because of important business decision and oversight responsibilities, a director has both legal and customary rights of access to the information and resources needed to do the job. Among the most important are the rights to:

- inspect books and records;
- request additional information reasonably necessary to exercise informed oversight and make careful decisions;
- inspect facilities as reasonably appropriate to gain an understanding of the operations of the business;

- receive timely notice of all meetings in which a director is entitled to participate;
- receive copies of key documents and of all board and committee meeting minutes; and
- receive regular oral or written reports of the activities of all board committees.

In addition, within reasonable time and manner constraints, a director generally has the right of access to key executives and other employees of the corporation and to the corporation's legal counsel and other advisors to obtain information relevant to the performance of the director's duties. A director should always be able to request that any issue of concern be put on the board (or appropriate committee) agenda.

A director's right to information is accompanied by the duty to keep corporate information confidential and not to misuse that information for personal benefit or for the benefit of others.

The board and board committees should expect the general counsel to be available as a resource to advise them as they see fit. Correspondingly, the general counsel must recognize that the client is the corporation, as represented by the board of directors, and not the CEO or any other officer or group of managers. The board and board committees should also have access to the corporation's regular outside counsel and the authority to retain their own legal counsel and professional advisors, independent of those who usually advise the corporation, when they determine such independent advice is desirable. Indeed, the Sarbanes-Oxley Act grants the audit committee the authority to engage independent counsel and other advisors and requires the corporation to pay for these advisors.

C. Legal Obligations

The baseline standard for director conduct is that every director must discharge director duties in good faith and in a manner that the director reasonably believes to be in the best interests of the corporation. The director owes a "duty of loyalty" to the corporation, which requires acting in good faith and avoiding personal and financial conflicts with the corporation. A director must also act with the care that a person in a like position would reasonably believe appropriate under similar circumstances. Thus, a director must act in a prudent manner for the benefit of the corporation, viewed in light of the director's knowledge and experience and the situation at hand. This is often referred to as the "duty of care."

A director's duties of care and loyalty are based on the following concepts:

- *Acting in good faith*—acting honestly and dealing fairly; in contrast, a lack of good faith would be evidenced by acting, or causing the corporation to act, for the director's personal benefit, or acting intentionally with a purpose other than that of advancing the best interest of the corporation, or acting with the intent to violate applicable law, or failing to act in the face of a known duty to act, in a manner that demonstrates an intentional disregard of, or extreme inattention to, the director's duties;
- *Reasonably believes*—although a director's personal belief is subjective, the qualification that it must be reasonable— that is, based upon a rational analysis of the situation understandable to others—makes the standard of required conduct also objective, not just subjective;
- *Best interests of the corporation*—emphasizing the director's obligation to the corporation and the requirement to avoid acting in a self-interested manner to the corporation's detriment;
- *Care*—expressing the need to pay attention, to ask questions, to act diligently in order to become and remain generally informed and, when appropriate, to bring relevant information to the attention of the other directors; in particular, these activities include reading materials and engaging in other preparation in advance of meetings, asking questions of management or advisors, requesting legal or other expert advice when desirable for a board decision until satisfied that all information significant to a decision is available to the board and has been considered, and when relevant, bringing the director's own knowledge and experience to bear;

- *Person in a like position*—avoiding the implication of special qualifications and incorporating the basic attributes of common sense, practical wisdom, and informed judgment generally associated with the position of corporate director; and
- *Under similar circumstances*—recognizing that the nature and extent of the preparation for and deliberations leading up to decision making and that the level of oversight will vary, depending on the corporation's circumstances and the nature of the decision to be made.

1. Duty of Care

A director's duty of care primarily relates to the responsibility to become informed in making decisions and overseeing the management of the corporation. In meeting the duty of care, a director should consider the following:

a. Time Commitment and Regular Attendance

A director is expected to commit the required time to prepare for, attend regularly, and participate (in person when feasible) in board and committee meetings. A director may not participate or vote by proxy; personal participation is required (which may take place by telephone or video when in-person participation is not possible).

b. Need to Be Informed and Prepared

In most (if not all) cases, the best source of information about the corporation is management. Management must provide directors with sufficient information to keep them properly informed about the corporation's business and affairs, and directors should not be reluctant to request additional information in order to be sufficiently informed and prepared. Without sufficient information, directors cannot participate meaningfully or fulfill their duties effectively.

When specific actions are contemplated, directors should receive the relevant information far enough in advance of the board or committee meeting to study and reflect on the issues raised. Important, time-sensitive materials that become available between meetings should be promptly distributed to directors. On their part, directors should review carefully the materials supplied. If a director believes that information is insufficient or inaccurate or is not made available in a timely manner, the director should (absent exigent circumstances) request that action be delayed until appropriate information is made available and can be studied, if possible under the circumstances. If a director believes that expert advice would be desirable in forming a decision, the director should request that the board seek such advice. If a director believes the board is repeatedly not timely provided with the appropriate information to enable the director to act in an informed manner, and is unsuccessful in efforts to obtain information, the director should urge the board to consider steps to remedy the situation. If such changes do not occur, the director should consider resigning.

c. Right to Rely on Others

In discharging board or committee duties, a director is entitled by law to rely in good faith on management and on the board committees on which the director does not serve to perform their delegated responsibilities. A director is also entitled to rely in good faith on reports, opinions, information, and statements (including

> In discharging board or committee duties, a director is entitled by law to rely in good faith on management and on the board committees to perform their delegated responsibilities.

financial statements and other financial data) presented by (i) the corporation's officers or employees whom the director reasonably believes to be reliable and competent in the matters presented; (ii) legal counsel, public accountants, or other persons as to matters that the director reasonably believes to be within their professional or expert competence or as to which the person otherwise merits confidence; and (iii) committees of the board on which the director does not serve. Such reliance is permissible unless the director has knowledge that would make the reliance unwarranted. Delegation to a committee does not relieve a director of oversight responsibility. A director who relies on others to whom work has been delegated should keep reasonably informed about their efforts.

Directors also implicitly rely on each other's statements, good faith, and judgment in making decisions for the benefit of the corporation. Such reliance is particularly likely when some directors have substantial experience or expertise in an area germane to the corporation's business—for example, by having specialized knowledge about a particular industry. Although the standards of director conduct do not vary depending on the special qualifications of individual directors, directors are expected to use their knowledge, experience, and special expertise for the benefit of all directors and the corporation generally.

Obtaining input from competent advisors is a hallmark of a careful decision-making process. For this reason, directors who rely in good faith on advisors, professionals, and other persons with particular expertise or competence generally enjoy broad protections from liability if the directors' business decisions are challenged. Nevertheless, the directors have the final responsibility for their actions.

d. Inquiry

When directors uncover or receive information indicating that the corporation is or may be experiencing significant problems or may be engaging in unlawful conduct, they should make further inquiry, particularly with respect to the reliability or accuracy of this information, and follow up until they are reasonably satisfied that management is dealing with the situation appropriately.

A director should inquire into potential problems or issues when alerted by circumstances or events suggesting that board attention is appropriate. For example, inquiry is warranted when information provided on an important matter appears materially inaccurate or inadequate or when there is reason to question the competence, loyalty, or candor of management or of an advisor. When directors uncover or receive information indicating that the corporation is or may be experiencing significant problems or may be engaging in unlawful conduct, they should make further inquiry, particularly with respect to the reliability or accuracy of this information, and follow up until they are reasonably satisfied that management is dealing with the situation appropriately. Even when there are no red flags, directors should satisfy themselves periodically that the corporation maintains procedures that are appropriately designed to identify and manage business risks and are reasonably effective in maintaining compliance with laws and corporate policies and procedures.

e. Disclosure among Directors

It is important that there be candid discussion among the directors and between directors and management. Each director must disclose to other directors information known to the director to be material to the decision-making or oversight responsibilities of the board or its committees. Directors occasionally also have legal or other duties of confidentiality owed to another corporation or entity. When such a situation arises, the director should seek legal advice regarding the director's obligations, which ordinarily would include reporting to the other directors the existence of the confidentiality obligations and not participating in consideration of the matter.

2. Duty of Loyalty

The duty of loyalty requires a director to act in good faith and in the best interests of the corporation—and not in the director's own interest or in the interest of another person (e.g., a family member or potential competitor) or organization with which the director is associated. There is a variety of situations in which a director's loyalty to the corporation can be questioned. These situations fall into two basic categories. The first involves situations in which a director's personal financial interest conflicts with that of the corporation. The second involves situations in which a director acts in a manner that is disloyal to the corporation for a reason other than a financial conflict of interest.

Breaches of this duty may include taking action (or refraining from taking action) for a purpose other than advancing the best interests of the corporation. In this regard, a director's failure to attend to his or her duties can be so egregious as to give rise to an inference that the director intentionally or knowingly is disregarding these duties or responsibilities, particularly when there appears to be a conscious disregard of the potential harm to the corporation. A director also may breach the duty of loyalty by intentionally causing the corporation to violate applicable law, thereby subjecting the corporation to the possibility of criminal and civil penalties.

a. Acting in Good Faith

The fundamental requirement of loyalty is that a director must believe in good faith that the director's actions are in the best interests of the corporation. Directors can fail to act in good faith in a variety of ways. For example, directors who act intentionally with a purpose other than advancing the corporation's interests fail to act in good faith, or who fail to act when there is a known duty to act may fail to meet their good faith obligations. Directors who act with the intent to violate or with intentional disregard of an applicable law, or who fail to cause the corporation to establish internal controls or monitoring and compliance systems, or who fail to respond to red flags may also fail to act in good faith. When a director can be perceived as having a motive other than that of advancing the corporation's best interests, the director should consider whether recusal from the discussion and/or the vote on a particular subject would be appropriate.

b. Conflicts of Interest

A director should not use his or her corporate position for personal profit or gain or for any other personal or non-corporate advantage and should refrain from engaging in any transaction with the corporation on the other side unless the underlying action is demonstrably fair or has been approved by the disinterested directors or shareholders of the corporation after full disclosure. Each director should be alert and sensitive to any interest the director may have that might conflict with the best interests of the corporation. When a director has a direct or indirect financial or personal interest in a contract or transaction to which the corporation is to be a party—or contemplates entering into a transaction that involves use of corporate assets or may involve competition with the corporation— the director is considered to be "interested" in the matter.

A director should not use his or her corporate position for personal profit or gain or for any other personal or non-corporate advantage and should refrain from engaging in any transaction with the corporation on the other side unless the underlying action is demonstrably fair or has been approved by the disinterested directors or shareholders of the corporation after full disclosure.

An interested director should disclose the director's interest to the board members who are to act on the matter and disclose the relevant facts concerning the matter known to the interested director. Sometimes a conflict arises from a corporation's plan to do business with an entity with which a director has a preexisting relationship. The director, upon learning of such a conflict, should fully disclose the director's relationship and other pertinent information. If the confidentiality obligations a director owes to a third party impair or proscribe such disclosure, the director may not be able to discharge the director's duties to the corporation and may need to be recused from all participation concerning the matter or even resign.

In most situations, after disclosing the interest, describing the relevant facts, and responding to any questions, an interested director should leave the meeting while the disinterested directors complete their deliberations. This enables the disinterested directors to discuss the matter without being (or creating the appearance of being) influenced by the presence of the interested director. Directors should generally abstain from voting on matters in which they have a conflict of interest. Disclosures of conflicts of interest and the results of the disinterested directors' consideration of the matter should be documented in minutes or reports of the action taken. In some cases, it may be appropriate to form a special committee of disinterested directors to review and pass on the transaction.

Transactions that present conflicts of interest sometimes are unavoidable and are not inherently improper. These transactions may be properly authorized so long as they are approved by disinterested directors or shareholders after full disclosure of material information about the transaction. State corporation statutes usually provide procedures for authorizing or ratifying interested director transactions, and those procedures should be followed to safeguard both the corporation and the interested director and to protect the enforceability of any action taken. Notwithstanding such approval, if the transaction is challenged, the interested director is entitled to establish the entire fairness of the transaction to the corporation, judged according to circumstances at the time of the commitment.

A transaction between a director, or the director's immediate family, and the corporation is deemed a "related person" transaction under the federal securities laws and may have to be publicly disclosed in the corporation's annual report, proxy statement, or other public filings. Even if the transaction does not require public disclosure, the corporation may be required to disclose in general terms whether the board considered the transaction in determining whether the director is an "independent" director under market listing standards. Accordingly, the disinterested directors should consider the ramifications of such disclosures when voting on the transaction.

c. *Fairness to the Corporation*

Disinterested directors reviewing the fairness of a transaction having conflict of interest or self-dealing elements essentially seek to determine (i) whether the terms of the proposed transaction are at least as favorable to the corporation and its shareholders as might be available from unrelated persons or entities; (ii) whether the proposed transaction is reasonably likely to further the corporation's business activities; and (iii) whether the process by which the decision is approved or ratified is fair. If the shareholders could be adversely affected by the transaction, the directors should be especially concerned that those shareholders receive fair treatment. This concern is heightened when one or more directors or a dominant shareholder or shareholder group have a divergent or conflicting interest.

d. Independent Advice

Independent advice regarding the merits of a related person transaction is often helpful, particularly when a transaction is significant to the corporation. This advice may be contained in oral or written fairness opinions, appraisals, or valuations by investment bankers or appraisers; in legal advice or opinions on various issues; or in analyses, reports, or recommendations by other relevant experts.

e. Corporate Opportunity

The duty of loyalty is also implicated when a business opportunity related to the business of the corporation, including its subsidiaries and affiliates, becomes available to a director. The director must typically make it available to the corporation before the director may pursue the opportunity for the director's own or another's account. Whether this opportunity must first be offered to the corporation will often depend upon factors such as whether the opportunity is similar to the corporation's existing or contemplated business, the circumstances in which the director learned of the opportunity, and whether the corporation has an interest or expectancy in the opportunity.

If a director has reason to believe that a contemplated transaction might be a corporate opportunity, the director should bring it to the attention of the board and disclose the material information that the director knows about the opportunity. If the board, acting through its disinterested directors, disclaims interest in the opportunity on behalf of the corporation, then the director is free to pursue it.

3. Business Judgment Rule

If a board's decision is challenged in court by a claimant asserting deficient conduct, judicial review of the matter will normally be governed by the "business judgment rule." The business judgment rule is not a description of a duty or a standard for determining whether a breach of duty has occurred; rather, it is a standard of judicial review used in analyzing director conduct to determine whether a board decision can be subject to challenge or a director should be held personally liable.

The business judgment rule presumes that in making a business decision, disinterested directors acted on an informed basis, in good faith, and in the honest belief that the action taken was in the best interests of the corporation. Applying the rule in suits brought against directors by shareholders acting for themselves or derivatively on behalf of the corporation, the court will look to determine only whether the directors—at least those directors making the decision—were disinterested in the matter, appropriately informed themselves before taking the action, and acted in the good faith belief that the decision was in the best interests of the corporation. If so, the decision will not be second-guessed, and the directors will be protected from personal liability to the corporation and its shareholders, even if the board's decision turns out to be unwise or the results of the decision are unsuccessful. The business judgment rule can protect both decisions to take action and decisions to take no action.

4. Duty of Disclosure

As fiduciaries, directors have an obligation to take reasonable steps to ensure that shareholders are furnished with all relevant material information known to the directors when they present shareholders with a voting or investment decision. Likewise, directors also have the duty to inform their fellow directors and management about information known to the director that is relevant to corporate decisions. Some courts have decided that even where the directors are not recommending shareholder action, they have a duty (independent of disclosure obligations generally under the federal securities laws) not to mislead or misinform shareholders.

5. Confidentiality

A director must keep confidential all matters involving the corporation that have not been disclosed to the public. Directors must be aware of the corporation's confidentiality, insider trading, and disclosure policies and comply with them. Although a public company director may receive inquiries from major shareholders, the media, analysts, or friends to comment on sensitive issues, particularly with respect to business strategy or financial information, an individual director is not usually authorized to be a spokesperson for the corporation. Directors should avoid responding to such inquiries, particularly when confidential or market-sensitive information is involved, and they should instead refer requests for information to the CEO or other individual designated by the corporation to deal with such inquiries.

A director must keep confidential all matters involving the corporation that have not been disclosed to the public. Directors must be aware of the corporation's confidentiality, insider trading, and disclosure policies and comply with them.

A director who improperly discloses nonpublic information to persons outside the corporation could harm the corporation's competitive position or damage investor relations and, if the information is material, could trigger personal liability as a tipper of inside information or cause the corporation to violate federal securities laws. Equally important, the unauthorized disclosure of nonpublic information by directors can damage the bond of trust between and among directors and management, discourage candid discussions, and jeopardize boardroom effectiveness and director collaboration.

6. Risk and Compliance Oversight

In connection with overseeing the business and affairs of the corporation, a director should also assess whether the corporation has established and implemented programs designed to address the following risk and compliance issues.

a. Risk Management

The board, or an appropriate committee, should receive periodic reports describing and assessing the corporation's programs for identifying financial, industry, and other business risks and for managing such risks to protect corporate assets and reputation. A full understanding of the controls and infrastructure for the prevention, mitigation, and remediation of risks allows a corporation to determine its risk/reward appetite and risk tolerance in various business areas and to manage those risks more effectively, thus enabling informed risk taking. Some corporations have designated a chief risk officer and/or created a high-level management committee on risk, which reports regularly to the board. Some corporations, especially those in the financial services sector, have board committees focused exclusively on risk. Crisis management, information technology security, insurance arrangements, compliance programs, plant security, protection of confidential information, and intellectual property are typical risk management programs.

b. Compliance with Law

The board is responsible for overseeing management's activities in assuring the corporation's compliance with legal requirements in the various jurisdictions in which the corporation does business. A well-conceived and properly implemented program of compliance can significantly reduce the incidence of violations of laws and corporate policy. It can also reduce or eliminate civil lawsuits, penalties, or prosecution against the corporation for violations of law that occur in spite of such a program. The federal sentencing guidelines greatly increase the penalties for corporations found guilty of criminal violations, yet

The federal sentencing guidelines greatly increase the penalties for corporations found guilty of criminal violations, yet provide for significant fine reductions for corporations with appropriate programs in place to prevent and detect violations of law. Thus, directors should periodically satisfy themselves that an appropriate process is in place to encourage attention to legal compliance issues and claims against the corporation and the timely reporting of significant legal or other compliance matters to the board or an appropriate board committee.

provide for significant fine reductions for corporations with appropriate programs in place to prevent and detect violations of law. Thus, directors should periodically satisfy themselves that an appropriate process is in place to encourage attention to legal compliance issues and claims against the corporation and the timely reporting of significant legal or other compliance matters to the board or an appropriate board committee.

Companies should have formal written policies designed to promote compliance with law and corporate policy, which should be periodically monitored for effectiveness, particularly if the corporation operates in an industry subject to laws and regulations that demand special compliance procedures and monitoring. Many public companies assign compliance oversight to the audit committee, which meets regularly with the company's general counsel or regular outside counsel to be briefed on compliance and claims. With the increased burdens placed on public company audit committees, some boards have elected to form a separate compliance or legal affairs committee. Directors should consider whether delegating oversight for multiple compliance issues to a single board committee is appropriate for the corporation's legal and regulatory compliance profile.

The board should receive reasonable assurances that employees of the corporation are informed and periodically reminded of corporate policies, including those pertaining to compliance with (i) codes of business conduct, (ii) anti-discrimination and employment laws, (iii) environmental and health and safety laws, (iv) anti-bribery laws, (v) antitrust and competition laws, and (vi) securities laws, particularly those addressing insider trading. The major securities markets require their listed companies to adopt codes of business conduct applicable to all employees, officers, and directors. The corporation should have appropriate controls, which may include whistle-blower and hotline policies, throughout the organization for monitoring compliance with such laws as well as with the corporation's code of business conduct and for addressing potential violations when they arise.

All persons involved in the compliance process should have direct access to the general counsel or other compliance officer so that sensitive compliance situations may be raised for prompt consideration. In addition, the board should consider whether the compliance program has adequate resources and authority to perform its function.

c. Quality of Disclosure

A corporation's disclosure documents (e.g., annual reports, quarterly reports, current reports, proxy statements, prospectuses, and earnings releases) must fairly present material information about the corporation and its business, financial condition, results, and prospects. Management is responsible for drafting and preparing the corporation's disclosures. The directors should, as part of their oversight function, be satisfied that the corporation's

> *Directors should be generally familiar with the corporation's more significant filings and be satisfied that the disclosure conveys the significant information about the business in an understandable manner. They also should be satisfied with the procedures the corporation has in place to ensure proper and timely disclosure.*

procedures for preparing these documents are reasonably designed to produce accurate and complete public disclosures. Directors should be generally familiar with the corporation's more significant filings and be satisfied that the disclosure conveys the significant information about the business in an understandable manner. They also should be satisfied with the procedures the corporation has in place to ensure proper and timely disclosure. Many public companies have established internal disclosure committees composed of managers who have specific responsibility for the company's SEC filings and other public financial disclosures.

d. Employee Safety, Health and Environmental Protection, and Product Safety

Although employee safety, health and environmental protection, and product safety are matters of legal compliance, they also involve public concerns and corporate values such as business reputation and employee health and morale. Compliance with environmental standards, whether government-mandated or self-imposed, is particularly important, because violations can in many cases have a material financial effect on the corporation, trigger state or federal civil or criminal investigations, and pose special problems of public safety. Global warming and being a "green company" are other examples of environmental issues that can affect business reputation, culture, and morale. The regular oversight by the board in this area often affects the corporation's attitude towards compliance because it sends a message that compliance is valued at the highest level of the corporation.

e. Political Activity

Corporate officers and employees frequently participate in the governmental process on behalf of the corporation by seeking to influence legislative activities, shape regulations, or encourage or prevent government action. The actions and political positions taken are often highly visible and may affect the reputation of the corporation. Accordingly, they should be monitored by the board or one of its committees, and in the first instance, by legal counsel, for there are often regulatory implications. In addition, federal law prohibits some political contributions by corporations and limits political contributions by individuals.

f. Crisis Management

In recent years, many corporations have adopted and familiarized their boards with crisis management programs designed to organize the response to a corporate crisis, such as a natural disaster, terrorist activities, civil unrest, or a significant adverse corporate development. Such programs address a variety of issues relating to an emergency, such as disseminating information both internally and to the public, providing for back-up systems and records, and following employee safety and business operation procedures during the emergency. Members of a crisis management team typically include outside counsel and other advisors. It may be appropriate to develop different kinds of crisis management programs and teams to respond to different kinds of potential emergencies. Board-level participation in monitoring the development of such programs provides an objective review of management's plans for response, lends credibility to the response, and assures that board members are appropriately informed.

D. Change-of-Control Transactions and Election Contests

The board of directors is generally expected to establish a corporation's long-term business strategy and the time frame for achieving corporate goals. Directors are free to consider the relative merits of various alternatives for the corporation over the short, medium, or long term, as appropriate.

> *The board of directors is generally expected to establish a corporation's long-term business strategy and the time frame for achieving corporate goals. Directors are free to consider the relative merits of various alternatives for the corporation over the short, medium, or long term, as appropriate.*

The sale of the corporation is one of the most important matters to come before a board. An outright sale of the company for cash ends the shareholders' ownership of the business, while a sale of the corporation for stock changes the form and substance of the shareholders' investment in the business. In deciding whether to sell the corporation, directors should consider not only the potential value of the transaction to shareholders (compared with other alternatives reasonably available to the corporation), but also the risks inherent in the transaction, including the risk that the transaction will not close. If the transaction is publicly announced but is delayed or not completed, the corporation risks losing valuable employees and disrupting relationships with key customers and suppliers. Although every change-of-control transaction presents this risk, directors should consider the relative likelihood of events that might result in a transaction being delayed or not closing, such as regulatory issues, and the possible mitigation of these risks.

Before a decision is made to sell control of the corporation, the directors must seek the best reasonably available price and terms and may need to put protective measures in place so that the board can seek the best available transaction. There is no single blueprint a board should follow. In most cases, the board is best served by engaging experienced advisors who are familiar with customary terms and the legal issues involved.

A potential sale of control of the corporation may present conflicts of interest for directors and officers who stand to benefit from change-of-control provisions or who have preexisting relationships with one or more potential acquirers or will become part of the acquiring group. In this situation, the board can continue to act, with the interested directors absenting themselves from the discussion. If an interested party is in a position to control the decision, a court may review the transaction to determine whether it is fair to the corporation and its disinterested shareholders. Where potential conflicts of interest are present, it is prudent to have independent and disinterested directors who are empowered to engage independent, qualified advisors, handle negotiations with the interested party. The corporation will likely have enhanced disclosure obligations under federal and state law in connection with a potential sale of the corporation.

Similarly, directors soliciting shareholder votes in an election contest will likely have enhanced disclosure obligations. Shareholders generally have the right to nominate proposed directors in accordance with the procedures set forth in the corporation's charter and bylaws. Incumbent directors faced with a hostile election contest may not take actions designed to frustrate shareholders' voting rights.

Because these situations have the potential to raise various strategic and financial issues, as well as complicated legal issues, directors are well served by obtaining advice from experienced counsel and qualified financial advisors.

E. Financial Distress Situations

The directors of a corporation facing potential default on obligations or bankruptcy must make decisions not encountered by the directors of financially healthy companies. Although directors' general responsibilities continue to apply, circumstances of severe financial distress can alter corporate goals and enhance creditors' rights vis-à-vis the corporation. If a corporation is in financial distress, decisions regarding dividends and other distributions, recapitalizations, reorganizations, and other major corporate actions should be considered by the board only with the benefit of legal advice from experienced counsel.

If a corporation is in financial distress, decisions regarding dividends and other distributions, recapitalizations, reorganizations, and other major corporate actions should be considered by the board only with the benefit of legal advice from experienced counsel.

Insolvency is a legally significant status of financial distress. A corporation may be considered insolvent where the fair value of the corporation's liabilities exceeds the fair value of its assets. Insolvency may also exist where the corporation is not able to pay its debts as they fall due in the ordinary course of business. Directors should seek the advice of management if there is any uncertainty whether the corporation is solvent and, when appropriate, hire professionals to assess a corporation's solvency.

Insolvency generally gives rise to additional legal protections to creditors. The laws of most states and the U.S. Bankruptcy Code prohibit transactions that may prejudice creditors' ability to obtain payment from the corporation. A corporation can be liable under these laws if it is in financial distress and transfers assets of value without receiving reasonably equivalent value in return. Similarly, various state laws and the U.S. Bankruptcy Code prohibit corporations from preferring some creditors over others. Directors who approve corporate action violating such laws, thereby resulting in harm to the corporation, may be subject to claims of personal liability for alleged breaches of legal duties.

The laws of many states also provide that directors of financially distressed corporations can be personally liable to the corporation or its creditors for causing the corporation to pay dividends or make other distributions to shareholders when insolvent. Notably, the current or imminent insolvency of a corporation implicates the director's duties in a subtle but important manner. Rather than managing the corporation to advance shareholder interests, the directors of an insolvent corporation must seek to maximize the value of the corporation so that the corporation can pay off as many of its legal obligations as possible. The reasoning behind this is straightforward: the corporation's first duty is to meet its legal obligations. When a corporation cannot do that, shareholders' interests become a secondary consideration.

Board Process, Structure, and Operations

Boards of directors should be organized and their proceedings conducted in ways that encourage, reinforce, and demonstrate the board's role as an independent and informed monitor of the conduct of the corporation's business and affairs and the performance of its management. No one governance structure fits all corporations, and there is

Boards of directors should be organized and their proceedings conducted in ways that encourage, reinforce, and demonstrate the board's role as an independent and informed monitor of the conduct of the corporation's business and affairs and the performance of its management.

considerable diversity of organizational structures. Each board should develop a governance structure that is appropriate for its circumstances.

Board process, structure, and operations, over time, will significantly affect the board's ability to exercise its powers and discharge its obligations effectively. This relationship is particularly strong in public companies, where the board of directors has a majority of independent directors; the independent directors, by definition, have a limited relationship with the corporation on whose board they sit; many, if not most, of these directors have competing demands for their time and attention; and the board has only a discrete amount of time to meet. In these circumstances, careful consideration must be paid to the "mechanics" of the board meeting. Otherwise, there is a real risk that directors will not use their time effectively to address and focus on the most important issues and work together in a productive manner.

The key contributions of directors are their time and talent. Boards should focus on the optimal deployment of those resources and avoid a "checklist" approach to addressing legally prescribed tasks. The board should determine and prioritize its most important duties and develop a structure and meeting schedule that optimizes the board's time and talents accordingly.

A. Board Composition—Qualifications and Independence

Elected by the shareholders at the shareholder meeting, the board has the power to appoint individuals to fill any vacancies on the board between shareholder meetings, nominate directors for reelection, and nominate individuals for election by shareholders as new directors. In determining board composition, directors should consider both the personal qualities of the individual directors and the overall mix of experience, independence, and diversity of backgrounds likely to make the board of directors, as a body, effective in monitoring and overseeing the performance of the corporation and contributing to its success.

If the board of directors of a public corporation is to function most effectively, it must exercise independent judgment in carrying out its responsibilities. Equally important, it must be perceived, by shareholders and other corporate constituencies, to be acting with independent judgment. The value of independent judgment is the ability to apply a healthy skepticism to management's reports and to focus primarily on creating value for shareholders. Consequently, the major securities markets require all listed companies to have a majority of "independent" directors, as defined by the markets—unless they are controlled companies, in which a majority of the voting power is held by a person or a group. The major securities markets also require, with limited exception, all members of the key oversight committees—audit, compensation, and nominating/corporate governance, or any committee to which these committees' duties are delegated—to qualify as "independent" directors. In addition, for all public companies, audit committee members must meet the separate definition of audit committee independence set forth in the Sarbanes-Oxley Act, which is, in some respects, more stringent than the major securities markets' definitions of director independence.

In general, a board can determine that a director is independent only if the director is free of any family relationship or any material business or professional relationship (other than stock ownership and the directorship) with the corporation or its management that would affect independence and has been free of any such relationship for at least three years. When making an independence determination, the board should consider all relevant facts and circumstances, and the board should review the materiality of a director's relationships with the corporation from both the director's standpoint and the standpoint of the individuals or organizations with which the director has an affiliation. Public corporations must disclose in their annual meeting proxy statements the names of the independent directors, as well as the principles underlying the independence determination and any transactions, relationships, or arrangements not otherwise disclosed that were considered by the board in determining whether the director is independent.

The major securities markets have identified the following relationships as being presumptively inconsistent with a director's independence:

- the director is a current or recent officer or employee of the corporation or any of its affiliated enterprises;
- the director has a business or professional relationship with the corporation, one of its affiliated enterprises, or one of its business partners that is material to the corporation or to the director;
- the director has a business or professional relationship with the corporation that involves significant dealings with senior management on a continuing basis, such as the relationship between the corporation and its investment bankers or legal counsel, even if the economic value

of the relationship is not material to the corporation or to the director;

- an executive officer of the corporation is serving on the compensation committee of the corporation that currently employs the director;
- the director has a current or recent affiliation with the corporation's external auditor; and
- an immediate family member of the director has any of the foregoing relationships.

It is important to note that the fact that a director is independent under the listing standards of a securities market does not mean that a director will be determined to be "disinterested" with respect to a particular decision. In reviewing director actions in conflict of interest situations or when a special board committee is established, courts are not limited by the board's determination that a director is independent and will look at the range of business, social, and personal relationships between directors participating in the decision and the corporation and its senior managers in determining whether such directors are in fact disinterested as to the particular decision.

B. Board Leadership

For many public companies in the United States, the CEO of the corporation also serves as chair of the board. In a growing number of public companies, however, the two functions are separated, with the chair providing leadership to the board, often serving as a liaison between the board and the CEO, and sometimes serving as a mentor to the CEO. Where the CEO also serves as board chair, a growing practice is to have the independent directors formally designate, among themselves, a director to act as a presiding or lead director. The chair of the nominating/corporate governance committee or a senior member of the board is often asked to act in that capacity. The presiding or lead director typically works with the CEO to prepare the board agenda and determine the types of information to be distributed to the board and its committees, presides at executive sessions of the non-management directors, and serves as the board's liaison to the CEO between meetings. The latter role is not intended to limit an individual director's ability to communicate directly with the CEO, however. The presiding or lead director may also be called upon by the board or by senior management to meet with shareholders or shareholder groups that wish to convey concerns to the board of directors. If such meetings are held, the full board should be promptly informed of such communications. The New York Stock Exchange (NYSE) requires listed companies to identify publicly, by name or position, the director or directors who preside at meetings of non-management directors and to inform shareholders how they may communicate with non-management directors.

C. Quality of Information

The quality of the information made available to directors will significantly affect their ability to perform their roles effectively. Because management is the primary source of information about the corporation, directors should insist that management provide them with information

> *The quality of the information made available to directors will significantly affect their ability to perform their roles effectively.*

that is (i) timely and relevant, (ii) concise and accurate, (iii) well organized, (iv) supported by any background or historical data necessary to place the information in context, and (v) designed to inform directors of material aspects of the corporation's business, performance, and prospects. Agenda-related information should be furnished to the directors sufficiently in advance of board or committee meetings to allow time for careful study and thoughtful reflection.

To get information from sources other than management, many boards receive analysts' reports about the corporation for outside perspective and analysis, as well as benchmarking data, which allow boards to make comparisons to other corporations in the same industry group or with similar characteristics. Increasingly, directors are communicating directly with senior-level employees and managers to learn more about the corporation's business, and some boards schedule site visits for the non-management directors so they can directly observe business operations and speak with employees at the operating level of the business.

D. Control of the Agenda

Traditionally, management has determined the presentations to be made and the matters to be acted on by the board, but that is less the case today. If there is a non-executive chair of the board or a presiding or lead director, that director and the CEO will often collaborate on the agenda and plans for the meeting. Any director can nonetheless request that an item be included on the agenda. Further, the board should satisfy itself that there is an overall annual agenda of matters that require recurring and focused attention, such as the achievement (as well as periodic reexamination and updating) of operational and financial plans, an evaluation of the performance of the CEO and other members of executive management, an evaluation of board and committee performance, and the adequacy and appropriateness of corporate systems and controls that address legal compliance, risk management, corporate policy supervision, financial controls, and timely and accurate financial reporting and other disclosures.

E. Legal Counsel

The board and each of its committees should generally look to the corporation's general counsel as the primary resource for legal analysis and advice. The general counsel's client is the corporation, as represented by the board of directors, not the CEO or any other officer or group of managers. For this reason, many boards or their audit committees meet regularly in a private session with the general counsel. In addition, the board and each of its committees should have access to the corporation's regular outside counsel if there is one and should have the authority to retain their own legal counsel and professional advisors, independent of those who usually advise the corporation. While a specific circumstance (e.g., allegations of management wrongdoing or negotiating executive pay packages) may prompt the board or, more likely, a board committee to seek independent advice, a board committee may choose to have regular outside counsel advise the committee generally in meeting its duties and responsibilities.

The board and each of its committees should generally look to the corporation's general counsel as the primary resource for legal analysis and advice. The general counsel's client is the corporation, as represented by the board of directors, not the CEO or any other officer or group of managers.

As part of their annual self-evaluations, the board and each of its committees should consider whether each is receiving appropriate advice as to legal and compliance requirements and timely updates on legal exposure. In addition, each should consider whether it has a good understanding of when it is desirable to seek legal advice from lawyers other than the general counsel and the outside lawyers regularly engaged by the corporation.

F. Number of Meetings and Scheduling of Meetings

The number of meetings a board finds necessary or useful varies with the size, complexity, and culture of the business enterprise. Some boards prefer more frequent, shorter meetings, whereas others prefer fewer, lengthier meetings. Some boards schedule one extended planning or strategic meeting each year and shorter meetings during the rest of the year. Boards of public companies should hold regularly scheduled meetings at least quarterly, typically tied to the release of quarterly financial information. Most public company boards schedule six to eight regular meetings a year and hold special meetings as needed.

Time at board and committee meetings should be scheduled carefully because the length of time budgeted for a meeting will limit the topics to be considered and the depth of the discussion at that meeting. Moreover, the time at a meeting should be balanced between management presentations and discussion among directors and management. If concise reports and analyses can be given effectively in writing, they should be so furnished in advance in order to facilitate discussion at the meeting.

G. Executive Sessions

The major securities markets require periodic meetings of the non-management directors in executive session (i.e., without management present), and many public companies hold an executive session of the non-management directors at every board meeting. These sessions can provide a forum for non-management directors to bring up ideas or raise issues they may otherwise be reluctant to raise in the full boardroom, to share candid views about management's performance, to discuss whether board operations are satisfactory, and to raise any potentially sensitive issues regarding specific members of management. These sessions are usually coordinated with meetings of the board and, if regularly scheduled, become routine and accepted by management.

If the CEO is also the board chair, most boards designate a director to convene and preside at these sessions. Executive sessions are most effective if they are planned in advance, with participants having a clear idea of the purpose of the session and the issues to be addressed. Following each session, either the director presiding at the session or the full group typically briefs the CEO on what was discussed and on whether any actions are to be taken as the result of the session.

Unless an executive session occurs during the course of a properly convened board meeting (which has not been adjourned) and a quorum is present, directors cannot take formal action on behalf of the board in executive session. For this reason, and to facilitate open and candid discussions regarding sensitive issues, detailed minutes of executive sessions need not be kept. Simple minutes that set forth the attendees at the executive session and generally list the topics discussed and recommended actions will normally suffice.

There are special occasions when the independent directors may wish to meet separately to consider management-sensitive issues, such as controversies involving senior management, a proposed change-of-control transaction, or a major change in management. Special advisors, such as special outside counsel, independent of the corporation's management, may be engaged in such cases to help the directors address the issue at hand.

H. Minutes, Note Taking, and Board Materials

All meetings of the board of directors and board committees—both regularly scheduled and special meetings—should be memorialized in minutes kept by the corporation. Minutes are important legal documents, reviewable by auditors in connection with their review of a corporation's financial statements as well as by shareholders for a proper purpose and, therefore, worthy of directors' attention and care. In addition, courts and regulatory bodies look to minutes of a meeting as evidence of what occurred at the meeting. Consequently, an experienced individual with good judgment should take minutes.

Minutes should contain, at a minimum, (i) the date and time of the meeting and a list of attendees; (ii) the topics discussed; (iii) any matters put to a vote and the outcome of any such vote (or a statement of decisions reached by consensus); (iv) whether any directors or other attendees abstained from voting or absented themselves from certain discussions at the meeting; (v) the material terms and rationale of any decision approved by the board or board committee; (vi) the individual responsible for preparing the minutes; and (vii) the time of adjournment.

Although different opinions exist about the appropriate level of detail included in the minutes, directors may reasonably insist that minutes be sufficiently detailed to support the availability of the protections provided by substantive law. This means summarizing important discussions and actions, but without purporting to provide a verbatim record or at-tributing specific words or points of view to particular directors. Corporation law generally protects disinterested and independent di-rectors from the threat of personal liability, provided that they act in good faith and consider pertinent information reasonably available to them. Minutes that do not reflect that an adequate deliberative process occurred may give rise to an inference that directors failed to consider pertinent information fully. Should directors be named as defendants in litigation, they may be compelled to explain their actions well after the fact and without the benefit of an adequate contemporaneous record of their deliberative process. Even if such directors are ultimately found not liable, they could be criticized for an inadequate deliberative process in making a business decision. Consequently, the minutes should aim to reflect the reality that the directors engaged in a deliberative process, taking into consideration the possible alternatives, and acted in what they reasonably believed to be the corporation's best interests.

> *Although different opinions exist about the appropriate level of detail included in the minutes, directors may reasonably insist that minutes be sufficiently detailed to support the availability of the protections provided by substantive law. This means summarizing important discussions and actions, but without purporting to provide a verbatim record or attributing specific words or points of view to particular directors.*

Note taking by directors implicates similar issues. Directors have no obligation to take notes. Those who do take notes to help them participate in a meeting should consider whether to retain them after the meeting. Because notes will not have been subject to a careful process of drafting, review, and approval, they may contain statements that are relatively easy to misinterpret or take out of context, particularly if produced in litigation. For example, notes may capture only part of a discussion or may not distinguish between words spoken and the note taker's thoughts. Consequently, directors generally should not retain notes after the formal minutes of a meeting are approved.

Furthermore, directors should confirm that the corporation maintains files containing the information provided to the board, such as board books and PowerPoint presentations. This information is helpful to demonstrate that the board made informed business judgments and to assist recollection if directors are questioned about past events. The corporation should develop, with board approval, a consistent policy for the retention of such information so that, together with quality minutes, there is a reliable record of the board's deliberations. Careful record keeping is also important if corporate records are ultimately produced to third parties.

Finally, the corporation's counsel should monitor the consistency of the corporation's approach to minutes and recordkeeping. With multiple committees and minute takers, inconsistencies in format and approval could arise that create issues in litigation or regulatory proceedings.

I. Board Evaluations

Directors of public companies are required by the major securities markets to evaluate, at least annually, the effectiveness of the board and each of its committees. As with executive sessions, board and board committee self-evaluations are most effective if they are planned in advance, with participants having a clear idea of the purpose of the self-evaluation and the issues to be addressed. Although self-evaluation can be done in a number of ways, many have found written questionnaires to be helpful as a basis for discussion when responses (oral or written) are collected in advance and made available at the session. External facilitators may also be helpful because of their experience with other companies and their independent perspective. Once the self-evaluation is completed, it is not necessary to retain copies of written responses to questionnaires, although maintaining a record of the process followed may be useful.

Evaluation of the performance of individual directors is generally conducted by or under the supervision of the nominating/corporate governance committee and is discussed separately in Section 8 of this publication.

J. Communications Outside the Boardroom

Outside of meetings, directors often have individual communications relating to the corporation with management or with other directors. Such one-on-one communications can be an efficient way to tap a particular director's expertise or point of view, and to some extent, these communications are inevitable.

Excessive outside communications about the corporation, however, particularly between management and a select group of directors, can lead to uneven knowledge among directors about important corporate issues and could impair the collective, inclusive, and candid exchange of views at board or committee meetings, or interfere with the board's collegial and independent relationship with management. Moreover, because official action by directors can occur only at a duly called meeting or by unanimous written consent, individual "polling" of directors will not be sufficient to authorize action requiring board approval. Regardless of any such individual communications among directors and officers, issues should be discussed fully and appropriately at timely meetings of the board as a whole or of a board committee.

K. Decision Making

Directors make decisions on a wide variety of matters, sometimes giving direction to management and other times approving major transactions. Some matters—such as changes in charter documents, authorization of dividends, election of officers, approval of mergers, financings, or corporate liquidations—generally require board action (as well as shareholder action, in some cases) as a matter of law. Directors are able to take formal action only at duly held meetings of the board or board committee or by unanimous written consent. It is advisable to use unanimous written consents only for routine matters.

When seeking approval of major actions, it is good practice to circulate in advance of the meeting summaries and supporting materials. Doing so will help to focus directors' attention on the precise actions proposed to be taken or authorized. Directors should be satisfied with the level of detail and the scope of the resolutions they approve.

Not all decisions by the board or board committees are formalized by the adoption of resolutions. Some may simply be a consensus or a "sense of the board" during the meeting to provide guidance to management. These types of decisions should be adequately described in the meeting's minutes to memorialize the decision and to avoid any misunderstanding among directors and management.

There may be occasions in which business constraints or a crisis requires important corporate decisions to be made promptly. A well-developed crisis plan and familiarity with the corporation can greatly enhance decision making in this context.

L. Disagreements and Resignation

Acting in the best interests of the corporation does not require that directors always unanimously agree on the best course of action. If, after a thorough discussion, a director disagrees with any significant action proposed to be taken by the board, the director should consider abstaining or voting against the proposal and consider requesting that the abstention or dissent be recorded in the meeting's minutes. Except in unusual circumstances, taking such a position should not cause a director to consider resigning. Resignations should be considered in instances where a director believes that management is not dealing with the directors, the shareholders, or the public in good faith or that the information being disclosed by the corporation is inadequate, incomplete, or incorrect. Directors may also consider resigning when they feel their point of view is being disregarded entirely. Public corporations are required to disclose director resignations in an SEC filing.

M. Time Commitment

Directors are expected to devote substantial time and attention to their responsibilities. Although directors' time commitment varies considerably (depending on the size and complexity of the enterprise and the issues being addressed at a particular time), the time required of directors of public companies is significant, particularly for members of the audit committee and the compensation committee. It is not uncommon for a director's total time commitment to involve 250 hours or more a year for meeting preparation, travel, meeting attendance, informal consultation with other board members and management, and regular review of materials to keep up with corporate developments.

Directors entertaining a new or continued board commitment should carefully consider how much time will be required to meet their responsibilities, particularly if they are members of the audit or compensation committees. Directors should not over-commit themselves, and the nominating/corporate governance committee should consider a board candidate's ability to devote the necessary time before determining to nominate the candidate.

In times of possible change-of-control transactions, financial distress, legal compliance violations, restatement of the financial statements, management succession crises, or similar circumstances, directors of public companies will be required to devote substantially more time.

N. Board Size

Each board should determine its own appropriate size to accommodate the corporation's needs, objectives, and circumstances. Factors that might influence board size are the corporation's need to meet applicable independence or other regulatory standards, to establish or maintain relationships with large shareholders or other constituencies, or to maintain a strong community presence. In accommodating these needs, board size should not be expanded to a point that interferes with effective functioning.

There is substantial variation in the size of boards of public corporations, with financial services corporations and corporations operating complex businesses typically having larger boards (as many as 15 or more members). The emerging consensus is that, except perhaps for the very largest and most complex corporations, smaller boards (7 to 11 members) function more effectively than larger boards. Directors serving on a smaller board typically will have more opportunities to participate actively in board deliberations, whereas larger boards can inhibit effective participation by individual members. Large boards address this participation issue through delegation of many significant activities to board committees.

Committees of the Board

Much of the work of the typical board of directors of a public company is performed in committee. Under the Sarbanes-Oxley Act and the major securities markets' listing standards, delegation of some significant matters must be made to board committees—in particular, the audit, compensation, and nominating/corporate governance committees—whose membership is limited to independent directors. Indeed, the independent board committee is at the core of many measures aimed at more effective corporate governance. In general, committees are useful when matters within the mandate of the committee require more time than can be dedicated to them at meetings of the full board, and when a smaller group of directors (who may have a particular interest or experience) focusing on specific issues may be more effective.

There is no universal mandate for a particular committee structure. Except for specific duties required to be delegated to committees of independent directors, some boards function almost entirely at the board level, whereas other boards act only upon broad strategy, policy guidance, and legally required matters, with monitoring and oversight handled mostly by committees. Each board needs to tailor committee functions and responsibilities to its own needs. In the case of regulated enterprises, particular committees may be required or encouraged by regulators (e.g., financial institutions may have board committees that specifically monitor the management of financial risks or oversee trust and fiduciary departments).

A. Standing Committees

The allocation of responsibilities among standing committees varies. For example, the audit committee often handles the primary review of legal compliance matters as part of its oversight of internal controls; in the alternative, the board may assign this review to another board committee or it may be maintained as a responsibility of the full board. Any discussion in this *Guidebook* that certain matters are generally considered by a particular committee is not meant to promote a particular board structure or any specific division of committee responsibilities.

Because of the delegation of key responsibilities to standing committees, a regular flow of reports and other information from the committees to the board is important to avoid a "balkanization" of board functions and to ensure that all directors are kept abreast of each committee's activities and significant decisions. For example, final minutes of all meetings of the standing committees are often provided to the full board, and the chairs of the committees should make regular reports. While the delegation to a committee of a given responsibility does not relieve the board of oversight responsibility over those functions, a director may rely upon the efforts and recommendations of a board committee on which the director does not serve, if the director reasonably believes reliance is warranted. The standards of conduct for a director in connection with committee service are the same as those for board service generally.

> *Because of the delegation of key responsibilities to standing committees, a regular flow of reports and other information from the committees to the board is important to avoid a "balkanization" of board functions and to ensure that all directors are kept abreast of each committee's activities and significant decisions.*

Here are basic guidelines and procedures on standing committee activity:

- *Committee composition*—Membership should be appropriate to the committee's purpose and, in the case of a public company, comply with federal law and securities market requirements. Membership considerations include relevant experience, expertise and, for members of the key oversight committees, independence from management and ability to meet significant time commitments.

- *Reporting to the board*—Standing committees should keep the board regularly informed of their activities through periodic oral reports at board meetings and circulation to all directors of committee agendas, meeting minutes, or written reports.

- *Legal limits of authority*—Committees must observe certain limits on their authority. The corporation statutes of most states prohibit committees from filling board vacancies, authorizing dividends or other distributions, and amending the corporation's bylaws.

- *Scope of delegation and responsibility*—The authority, function, and responsibilities of each committee should be clearly defined. In the past, this was typically done in bylaws or board resolutions. The major securities markets, however, require the duties of committees responsible for audit, compensation, and nominating/corporate governance matters to be specified in written charters, and the Sarbanes-Oxley Act requires specific duties, responsibilities, and powers to be assigned to the audit committee. In addition to the authority, function, and responsibilities of each committee, the charter or resolution may address committee membership qualifications, committee operations (including authority to delegate to subcommittees), reporting to the board, and the authority to engage outside advisors, including legal counsel.

- *Periodic review by the board*—The board or the nominating/corporate governance committee should review periodically the responsibilities assigned to each committee. This review should consider whether the assignments of duties and responsibilities continue to be appropriate and consistent with what each committee is actually doing and with each committee's meeting schedule (e.g., frequency and time allotted). As an example, if the audit committee meetings are regularly scheduled for just one hour before the board meeting, there likely will not be adequate time to cover the committee's agenda at some of those meetings.

B. Special and Other Committees

From time to time, the board may create a special committee to undertake special duties and responsibilities. In these instances, a board resolution or committee charter approved by the board, describing the scope of authority and the responsibilities assigned to the committee, should be adopted and included in the corporation's records. An example of a special committee is a committee of disinterested directors formed to consider transactions involving a potential conflict between the corporation and one or more of its officers, directors, or shareholders. This kind of ad hoc committee often determines to retain outside advisors, independent of any conflicted officers or directors. If each member of such committee is disinterested in the matter and able to exercise independent judgment, and the committee's processes are thorough, the risks of a successful challenge to the transaction and of director liability can be substantially reduced.

A special committee of disinterested directors may also be formed to consider transactions involving a potential conflict or to investigate potential litigation or wrongdoing. Special committees should be authorized to engage independent legal counsel and other advisors to help them determine the facts and an appropriate response to a potentially conflicting transaction or allegations of wrongdoing. The exact functions of such committees will depend upon the nature of the suspected wrongdoing, the apparent legal validity of any claims, the degree to which committee members are already familiar with the factual basis of the alleged wrongdoing, and the corporation's alleged involvement in the wrongdoing, if any. When an investigation is completed, the committee's counsel typically reports to

> *A special committee of disinterested directors may also be formed to consider transactions involving a potential conflict or to investigate potential litigation or wrongdoing. Special committees should be authorized to engage independent legal counsel and other advisors to help them determine the facts and an appropriate response to allegations of wrongdoing.*

the committee its conclusions regarding the validity of the potential claims, and may provide recommendations regarding how to proceed. Depending on the scope of authority delegated to the committee, the committee should then take appropriate action on behalf of the corporation or make a recommendation to the full board of directors.

Many boards of directors historically constituted executive committees of directors who were available to meet on important matters between regular meetings of the board. The need for such committees was based largely on the geographical dispersion of board members and the lack of easy communication tools. With modern telecommunications, use of executive committees has waned, in part, because the frequent use of such committees can have the effect of subordinating the roles of other directors to the members of the executive committee. If a board constitutes an executive committee, it should carefully consider the scope of the committee's authority.

Boards may create single-person board committees from time to time, if allowed under state law, to oversee or address specific areas, such as the pricing of a securities offering or other finance-related matters. Although single-person committees can be effective in time-sensitive and limited contexts, they are not widely used and difficulties may arise when the committee's responsibilities involve lengthy or more substantive tasks—such as in the conflict of interest or the investigation of wrongdoing situations outlined above—in which the deliberative efforts of multiple directors would be beneficial. Also, courts tend to be more wary about the independence of a single-person committee and may give less deference to its decisions. Consideration should be given to establishing an expiration date for ad hoc committees, especially single-person committees.

Audit Committee

The audit committee is a critical component of the corporate governance structure of public companies because it has general oversight responsibility for the public company's financial reporting process and internal controls. It also has the exclusive responsibility for retaining and overseeing the performance of the external auditor. For these reasons, the audit committee is an important part of the corporation's internal control, and as a result, the committee's performance will be evaluated by the external auditor in the course of its audit of the company's internal control over financial reporting under Section 404 of the Sarbanes-Oxley Act. In addition, the audit committee increasingly serves as a forum separate from management in which not only the internal and external auditors but also others, such as the corporation's legal counsel, can candidly report and discuss with the committee issues relating to accounting, auditing, financial reporting, and legal compliance matters. While public companies are required to have audit committees, private companies often have them as well, particularly when there are significant outside investors.

A. Principal Functions

Some duties and responsibilities of public company audit committees are established by federal law, SEC regulations, or securities market listing standards, and audit committees assume other functions as a matter of good practice. Current regulatory requirements mandate a formal, written charter specifying the committee's duties and responsibilities. The charter must be reviewed annually by the committee and published at least once every three years in the proxy statement sent to shareholders.

Audit committee members should understand the tasks specified in the committee's charter and evaluate whether each is performed. An audit committee will generally rely primarily on the corporation's accounting, finance, treasury, internal audit, and legal staffs, as well as the external auditor, for the information essential to the performance of its duties and responsibilities. The committee also has the authority to employ its own accountants, attorneys, or other advisors, and, under the Sarbanes-Oxley Act, the corporation must pay for these advisors. In light of the significant responsibilities delegated to the audit committee, some audit committees of public companies retain independent outside legal counsel to advise them on meeting their responsibilities. The advice of legal counsel can range from helping to identify the types of information that the audit committee should be reviewing and developing operational procedures and an annual schedule, to advising on disclosure, accounting, and internal control matters.

The following list sets forth duties for public companies' audit committees as required by SEC rules and securities market regulations. Audit committees of private companies may find this list useful in establishing the scope of their responsibilities and the content of their meetings.

Audit committees of public companies are required to:

- select and engage the corporation's external auditor and determine, for each fiscal year, whether to continue that relationship;
- review and approve annually the external auditor's fee arrangement and the proposed terms of its engagement, including the scope and plan of the audit;
- approve, before each engagement, any additional audit-related or non-audit services to be provided by the audit firm, based on the committee's judgment as to whether the firm is an appropriate choice to provide such additional services and whether the engagement would impair the firm's independence;

- establish procedures to receive and respond to any complaints or concerns regarding the corporation's accounting, internal controls, or auditing matters, including procedures for the confidential and anonymous submission by employees of any such complaints or concerns;
- serve as a channel of communication between the external auditor and the board and between the head of internal audit, if any, and the board;
- discuss the corporation's procedures for issuing quarterly and annual earnings press releases and for providing financial information and earnings guidance to analysts, the financial press, and rating agencies;
- review the corporation's annual and quarterly financial statements, and management certifications thereof, with management and the external auditor, and discuss with them the quality of management's accounting judgments in preparing the financial statements;
- review the Management's Discussion and Analysis section in each periodic report before filing with the SEC and discuss with management and the external auditor any questions or issues that arise in connection with that review;
- determine whether to recommend to the board that the audited annual financial statements be included in the corporation's annual report on Form 10-K to be filed with the SEC;
- review and approve the audit committee's annual report to shareholders required to be included in a public company's annual meeting proxy statement;
- receive and consider any required communications from the external auditor as a result of its timely review of the quarterly financial statements;
- consider, in consultation with the external auditor and the senior internal auditing executive, if any, the adequacy of the corporation's internal controls, which, among other things, must be designed to provide reasonable assurance that the corporation's books and records are accurate, that its assets are safeguarded, and that the publicly reported financial statements prepared by management are presented fairly in conformity with generally accepted accounting principles;

- review management's annual assessment of the effectiveness of the corporation's internal control over financial reporting and the external auditor's audit of internal control over financial reporting;
- meet periodically with management to review the corporation's major risk exposures and discuss the steps management has taken to monitor and control such exposures, such as risk-management programs and procedures and policies addressing legal compliance;
- review any related person transactions between the corporation and its officers or directors, or their family members or enterprises they control; and
- conduct an annual self-evaluation.

Other duties and responsibilities that many audit committees undertake as matters of good corporate practice include:

- establish a direct or dotted-line reporting relationship with the internal auditor, as the committee should have appropriate input in hiring and firing the head of internal audit, evaluating performance, and approving the internal audit plans and budget for the internal audit group;
- review the external auditor's management letter and management's responses thereto (the auditor's letter comments on any control deficiencies observed during the course of the audit and makes other recommendations arising from the audit);
- meet periodically with the corporation's disclosure committee or its representatives, if the corporation has such a committee; and
- if another committee does not do so, meet privately with the corporation's legal counsel or other key advisors from time to time to review the status of pending litigation, discuss possible loss contingencies, and review other legal concerns, including the corporation's procedures and policies addressing legal compliance and reduction of legal risk.

B. Membership

The audit committee of every public company must consist solely of directors who satisfy the independence requirements of both the company's securities market's listing standards and the federal securities laws, which provide that audit committee members may not receive any compensation from the corporation, such as consulting, advisory, or similar fees, other than their director and board committee fees and may not be affiliates of the corporation.

The major securities markets require a minimum of three members on the audit committee, and audit committees typically consist of three to five independent directors. The major securities markets also require that all committee members be financially literate and at least one member have accounting or financial management experience. In addition, under the Sarbanes-Oxley Act, a public company must disclose in its annual report to the SEC or annual meeting proxy statement whether any member of its audit committee qualifies as an "audit committee financial expert," a term defined by SEC regulation and focused on an individual's accounting and auditing knowledge and experience. If no member qualifies, then the corporation must state why the committee does not have such an expert. If the board determines that one or more of the committee's members qualify, then the corporation must disclose the name of at least one audit

In order to discharge their responsibilities, audit committee members should have a sufficient understanding of financial reporting and internal control principles to address material financial reporting and internal control issues. To support this oversight activity and as part of director continuing education, a growing number of public companies are providing audit committee members with professional advice on audit committee best practices and updates on important accounting issue developments.

committee financial expert and state whether that expert is independent. Because of this disclosure requirement, most public companies seek to have at least one member of the audit committee who qualifies as an audit committee financial expert. Any director who might be designated as an audit committee financial expert should be personally satisfied that the director in fact meets all of the requirements, which are quite stringent.

In order to discharge their responsibilities, audit committee members should have a sufficient understanding of financial reporting and internal control principles to address material financial reporting and internal control issues. To support this oversight activity and as part of director continuing education, a growing number of public companies are providing audit committee members with professional advice on audit committee best practices and updates on important accounting issue developments.

Regardless of these specific requirements, common sense, diligence, and an attitude of constructive skepticism are critical qualifications for an audit committee member.

C. Engaging the Auditors and Pre-approving Their Services

One of the key roles of the audit committee is engaging and supervising the company's external auditor. The audit committee must review and approve the terms of engagement for the auditor and must pre-approve all audit and non-audit services performed by the external auditor during the year, as well as any audit-related services performed by any other auditor. Many audit committees have developed policies and procedures to pre-approve specific and detailed types of audit and non-audit services before the need for an engagement arises. Notably, tax services and internal control-related services must be pre-approved, engagement by engagement. Some committees have delegated this pre-approval authority to the chair (or other members) of the audit committee to assure that necessary accounting work can proceed efficiently should the need for the services arise between meetings. The pre-approval process is intended to assure that the audit committee considers the effect of any audit and non-audit work on the auditor's independence. The audit committee also reviews the hiring of any former personnel of the auditor to assure that the hiring meets regulatory restrictions and that it will not affect the auditor's independence.

The audit committee of a public company must receive annually from its external auditor a letter as to the auditor's independence. The committee must discuss this letter with its auditor and consider what effect, if any, non-audit services provided by the external auditor will have on the auditor's independence.

D. Overseeing the Independent Audit

The audit committee should meet with the corporation's external auditor during the planning phase of each annual audit to review the planning, staffing, scope, and cost of the audit and to discuss any particular areas that may require emphasis or special procedures during the audit. After completion of the audit, the audit committee should review with the external auditor any problems or difficulties encountered by the external auditor, any significant issues that required discussion or involved debate with management during the course, or after completion, of the audit, and any letter summarizing audit observations provided to management by the external auditor together with management's response to that letter. With respect to any special audit procedures, the audit committee should review the findings of the external auditor and determine, with advisors' assistance as appropriate, whether any revisions to particular corporate policies or procedures are indicated.

The audit committee should understand when significant accounting judgments and estimates have been made that materially affect the corporation's financial statements. Because corporations sometimes have a choice among several available generally accepted accounting principles or practices to use in the preparation of financial statements, the committee should inquire into the effect that alternative choices would have had on reported results. The audit committee should review, at least annually, with the external auditor and with the chief financial officer (CFO) or chief accounting officer (CAO), major issues regarding, and any changes in, choices of accounting principles. In doing so, some audit committees find it useful to ask the external auditor to indicate to the committee what changes, if any, would have been made in the financial statements if the auditor, rather than management, had been responsible for preparing them. The committee is also required to review with the auditor the quality of management's accounting judgments.

The audit committee should review, at least annually, with the external auditor and with the chief financial officer or chief accounting officer, major issues regarding, and any changes in, choices of accounting principles. In doing so, some audit committees find it useful to ask the external auditor to indicate to the committee what changes, if any, would have been made in the financial statements if the auditor, rather than management, had been responsible for preparing them.

The committee also should discuss, often with the participation of the internal auditor, any significant deficiencies or material weaknesses identified by the auditor during the course of its annual internal control audit. If the auditor identifies any significant deficiencies or material weaknesses in the company's internal control over financial reporting, then the committee should oversee management's remediation of those control deficiencies. Failure to do so may cause the auditor to conclude that the audit committee itself constitutes a material weakness in the company's internal control because of its failure to oversee the remediation of significant deficiencies or material weaknesses in a timely manner.

Based on and relying upon these processes and reviews, the audit committee must determine whether to recommend to the board inclusion of the audited financial statements in the corporation's annual report on Form 10-K to be filed with the SEC.

E. Internal Audit

Most large public companies have an internal audit function, and the NYSE requires its listed companies to have an internal audit function. The internal auditors are typically employees of the corporation, although sometimes a corporation will out-source some or all of this function.

If an internal audit department exists, the audit committee should routinely meet, in private, with the senior internal audit-ing executive to discuss the relationship between the internal and external audit programs, to consider any special problems or issues that may have been encountered since their last meet-ing, and to review the implementation of any recommended cor-rective actions. The committee should also review the annual internal audit plan.

If the corporation does not have an internal audit function, the committee should consider with management and the exter-nal auditor whether such a function should be established and, if not, how the benefits and protections normally obtained from an internal audit function can otherwise be obtained. If the internal audit function has been outsourced, the committee should meet with appropriate representatives of that firm on a regular basis, including meeting in executive session.

F. Meetings with Auditors

Most meetings with external and internal auditors will be con-ducted in the presence of the CFO or CAO or other members of management responsible for financial affairs. Importantly, the NYSE requires its listed companies' audit committees to meet periodically with the external auditor and the head of the inter-nal audit staff, if one exists, separately, in executive session with-out the participation of other management. Typically, in these sessions, the auditors are asked whether (i) there are any matters regarding the corporation and its financial affairs and records that make the auditors uncomfortable, (ii) the auditors have had any significant disagreement with management, (iii) the audi-tors have had full cooperation of management, (iv) reasonably effective accounting systems and controls are in place, and (v) there are any material systems or controls or financial staffing areas that need strengthening. Many committees find it useful to have the external auditor describe the two or three issues that involved the most discussion with management during the course of the auditor's work. Correspondingly, the committee may also meet privately with management to discuss the quality of service provided by the external and internal auditors.

The audit committee should discuss with the external auditor and management the committee's role in reviewing quarterly financial reports. They should also discuss the procedure by which the external auditor can raise with the committee or its chair significant deficiencies or material weaknesses that come to the external auditor's attention during its audit work or during its mandated timely review of the quarterly financial statements.

The external auditor is required to assess whether the audit committee understands and exercises its oversight responsibility over financial reporting and internal controls as part of the auditor's annual audit of the corporation's internal control over financial reporting. As part of this assessment, the external auditor will consider its interaction with the audit committee, including the audit committee's knowledge about the corporation's accounting policies and internal controls and its monitoring of any control remediation efforts by management. If the auditor concludes that the audit committee's oversight is ineffective, then the auditor is required to report that conclusion, in writing, to the full board.

> *The external auditor is required to assess whether the audit committee understands and exercises its oversight responsibility over financial reporting and internal controls as part of the auditor's annual audit of the corporation's internal control over financial reporting.*

G. Meeting with Compliance Officers

The audit committee, unless there is another board committee responsible for such matters, should meet regularly with the officers responsible for implementing the corporation's codes of business conduct and compliance policies. Officers with compliance responsibilities typically include the corporation's general counsel, chief internal audit officer, and chief compliance officer. These officers often have the opportunity to meet with the committee outside the presence of any other executive officer or any director who is not independent to facilitate candid discussions with the committee. In any event, the responsible officers should report to the committee periodically, and the scope and content of such reports should be designed to give the committee, on a timely basis, information about material violations of law or corporate policies by senior managers or other personnel, and the discipline imposed, as well as information that will allow the committee to monitor the effectiveness of the overall compliance program. In addition, the general counsel should meet regularly with the audit committee, or another committee of independent directors, to communicate concerns regarding legal compliance matters, including potential or ongoing material violations of law by the corporation and breaches of duty by senior managers.

H. Establishing Procedures to Handle Complaints

The audit committee of a public company must establish procedures by which employees and others can report—on an anonymous and confidential basis, if so desired—concerns or complaints about accounting, internal control, and auditing matters. As audit committee members are not usually in the best position to conduct fact-finding or even to receive complaints or concerns in the first instance, the committee should create, with management's assistance, procedures adequate to ensure that information reaches the committee in a form, such as a summary or report, conducive to the identification of red flags and to a timely and efficient review and resolution by the committee. For example, the audit committee may decide to rely on an ethics or compliance officer to review and filter this information or may decide to outsource this task to a third-party service provider.

In addition, lawyers for public companies (both internal and outside counsel) may, in some cases, be required to report to a committee of independent directors, or to the board, credible evidence that a material violation of securities laws, breach of fiduciary duty, or similar violation by the issuer or any of its officers, directors, employees, or agents has occurred, is occurring, or is about to occur. Public companies may determine that the audit committee is the appropriate committee to receive any such reports. If so, the audit committee should have in place a process for receiving, considering, and acting upon such reports, including a standing arrangement for the committee to obtain legal advice from outside counsel as to how to proceed.

I. Meetings and Compensation

The audit committee should discuss and determine the number of meetings it needs to hold annually in order to deal effectively with its responsibilities. In light of the fact that the major securities markets' listing standards require audit committees to review quarterly and annual reports filed with the SEC, an audit committee should meet at least four times a year. Moreover, it is common for public company audit committees to have an in-person or video or telephone meeting with the company's CEO, senior financial managers, and external auditor in advance of each quarterly or annual earnings release, which are usually issued before quarterly and annual reports are completed. As a result, many audit committees schedule five to eight meetings a year, although some of these meetings may be by video or telephone conference.

When the committee does meet, it is important that other board scheduling not unduly limit the time for committee deliberations. Participating in committee meetings requires significant commitments of time on the part of the committee members. In view of the time and attention needed for committee affairs, the board, or its compensation or nominating/corporate governance committee, may want to consider providing the chair of the audit committee or other audit committee members with a higher level of compensation than provided to other board members. Some boards have done this, while others have determined that differential compensation among board members can create risks of divisions within the board and makes selection of members and rotation of committee assignments more difficult.

Compensation Committee

Executive compensation plays a central role in attracting, retaining, and motivating the management talent that is critical to the corporation's success. The compensation committee is responsible for approving executive compensation and, in many cases, for overseeing the planning for management succession. The integrity and transparency of this committee's decision-making process are of paramount concern to shareholders and regulators alike. Real abuses and perceived excesses in executive compensation (which includes compensation policies, plans, and programs) at some notable public companies led to many of the corporate governance reforms found in the Sarbanes-Oxley Act, and the recent spate of investigations focusing on the backdating of stock option grants ensures that regulatory and shareholder interest in executive compensation will not wane. Investors' desire for greater transparency in executive compensation in general and compensation committee decision making in particular resulted in the SEC's complete overhaul, in 2006, of the proxy disclosure requirements for executive compensation.

The executive compensation discussion—in both public and private forums—has generally focused on the following questions:

- Should the compensation packages for the CEO and other senior executives be established on an arm's length basis? If so, who should do the negotiating?
- Are the CEO and the other senior executives appropriately compensated?
- Is their compensation reasonably related to personal and corporate performance?

- Are severance and post-employment benefits properly related to corporate interests and reasonable in amount?
- Over time, are the compensation programs and policies attracting and retaining quality management for the corporation, and motivating the CEO and other senior managers to build long-term value for shareholders?
- Do a corporation's public disclosures about executive compensation give shareholders an accurate picture of how senior executives are being compensated and of the reasoning behind executive compensation decisions?

The committee needs to exercise its independent judgment to determine what compensation arrangements and levels are in the best interests of the corporation. When functioning effectively, the committee provides credibility and substance to the concept of independent oversight of executive compensation.

The compensation committee is at the center of this discussion. The committee needs to exercise its independent judgment to determine what compensation arrangements and levels are in the best interests of the corporation. When functioning effectively, the committee provides credibility and substance to the concept of independent oversight of executive compensation.

A. Membership

The compensation committee should and, in some instances, must consist solely of independent directors. The major securities markets generally require that independent directors make compensation decisions for executive officers, whether acting as a compensation committee or meeting in executive session. In addition, under the federal tax laws, decisions to pay any of the five most highly compensated executives more than $1 million annually must be made by directors who meet the Internal Revenue Service's definition of "outside director" in order for the compensation to qualify for a full federal tax deduction. Moreover, SEC rules exempt executive officer option grants from profit recapture only if the grant decisions are made by "non-employee directors," as defined in those rules. Each of these terms is similar to, but not the same as, the "independent director" definitions in securities market listing standards. Consequently, the eligibility of prospective committee members should be reviewed against each of these standards. Interlocking compensation committee memberships are strongly discouraged, trigger additional proxy statement disclosures, and may disqualify a director from being considered independent under securities market listing standards.

Apart from legal considerations, the committee's independence from management gives credibility to the compensation committee's key responsibility, which is to establish and approve compensation for executive officers on behalf of the corporation. With respect to the compensation for the CEO, even when a director meets the independence requirements of the applicable market's listing standards, if there are close personal or business ties between the director and the CEO, the director may not be an appropriate choice for membership on the compensation committee. As with board membership generally, diverse backgrounds and experiences can provide useful perspectives in committee deliberations.

B. Principal Functions

The compensation committee should:

- oversee the corporation's overall compensation structure, philosophy, policies, and programs and assess whether they establish appropriate incentives for senior executives;
- review and approve corporate goals and objectives relevant to CEO and senior executive compensation and evaluate executive performance in light of those goals and objectives;
- establish the compensation and benefits of the CEO and senior executives;
- evaluate and approve any employment agreements with executive officers;

- establish and periodically review policies for the administration of executive compensation programs (including all equity-based plans);
- make recommendations to the board with respect to incentive compensation plans and equity-based plans generally;
- establish and periodically review policies in the area of senior management perquisites;
- review and be satisfied with management's Compensation Discussion and Analysis disclosure that is included in the corporation's annual meeting proxy statement and discuss with management any issues or questions that arise from that review;
- review and approve the annual report of the compensation committee that will be included in the annual meeting proxy statement; and
- conduct an annual self-evaluation.

1. Chief Executive Officer Compensation

The purpose of the major securities markets' requirement that independent directors establish the CEO's compensation is to promote—and, in fact, mandate—the exercise of independent judgment on this sensitive and important matter. At minimum, this exercise of independent judgment should result in the committee creating and following a process to reach an informed decision that is something more than rubber-stamping somebody else's recommen-

The exercise of independent judgment should result in the committee creating and following a process to reach an informed decision that is something more than rubber-stamping somebody else's recommendations—how much more, of course, depends on the committee's judgment, as well as the facts and circumstances of the situation.

dations—how much more, of course, depends on the committee's judgment, as well as the facts and circumstances of the situation.

A compensation committee should consider seriously the most effective process by which it can reach an independent and informed decision about the appropriateness of the amount and composition of the CEO's compensation package. The committee may benefit from engaging and collaborating with competent, experienced, and independent compensation consultants, who can assist the committee in collecting comparative data and in advising on the best arrangement for the corporation. Regardless of whether the committee engages outside consultants or counsel for assistance, the committee itself is ultimately responsible for approving the terms, the amounts, and the forms of compensation.

Arm's length dealing on compensation decisions—in which the compensation committee members are personally involved, and, if they deem it appropriate using the resources of independent advisors or consultants—gives credibility and substance to the concept of independent oversight of executive compensation. The extent or type of arm's length dealing can vary depending on the facts and circumstances; for example, an outsider

> *Arm's length dealing on compensation decisions—in which the compensation committee members are personally involved, and, if they deem it appropriate using the resources of advisors or consultants—gives credibility and substance to the concept of independent oversight of executive compensation.*

brought in to lead the company may warrant a different process than the lifelong insider who has led the company for 10 years. In addition, if the CEO engages his or her own lawyer to negotiate the terms of the employment agreement, the committee should consider how best to protect the corporation's interest in the process—for example, considering hiring its own independent counsel to help negotiate the agreement.

Although the CEO will often meet with the compensation committee, he or she should not be present during all of its deliberations. The same is true of the corporation's senior compensation or human resources executive. Both the reality and the appearance of independent oversight are important; therefore, it is wise to have at least some committee discussions on senior officer compensation matters occur without members of management present, and the compensation of the CEO should be considered by the committee in a private session, without the presence of the CEO or the CEO's subordinate officers.

2. *Structure and Components of Executive Compensation*

The compensation committee should be guided by the basic principle that a significant portion of an executive's compensation should be tied to the corporation's financial objectives and performance, with an appropriate balance between short-term pay and long-term incentives. The structure and components of an executive compensation package will vary among industries and among companies. While benchmarking against peer companies is sometimes used as a tool to help determine executive compensation, the corporation should avoid simply matching or exceeding the compensation structure of peer companies. Company size, financial condition, industry characteristics, competitive factors, location, and corporate culture are all relevant factors for the committee in identifying a corporation's "peer" companies.

> *The compensation committee should be guided by the basic principle that a significant portion of an executive's compensation should be tied to the corporation's financial objectives and performance, with an appropriate balance between short-term pay and long-term incentives.*

In considering equity incentives, committees have a wide variety of tools, such as stock options, restricted stock, restricted stock units, stock appreciation rights, and other types of equity compensation. Although stock options were commonly used in years past because there was no charge to earnings associated with the grant of "at the market" stock options, recent changes to the accounting rules require companies to recognize the cost of stock options, thereby eliminating the accounting benefit of issuing options as compared to other forms of equity compensation. Consequently, many committees are considering granting other forms of equity compensation, such as restricted stock or restricted stock units, or options whose exercise price is indexed to corporate performance as compared against market indices or a peer group, or awards that vest only when specified performance goals are met. Committees are also requiring retention or holding periods for stock, whether granted or obtained on option exercise, in order to align executive pay more effectively with long-term performance. Some companies also establish stock ownership targets to further align the executives' interests with those of shareholders.

The committee should also review the benefits and perquisites provided to senior executives, particularly when approving employment contracts. Perquisites, or "perks," have received considerable attention due to excesses in their use, such as personal use of corporate aircraft. As a result, the SEC requires enhanced disclosure of perks. Another important area of scrutiny is benefits provided upon retirement or other termination of employment. There is widespread shareholder concern that these benefits are not sufficiently related to job performance and could be viewed as excessive when fully disclosed.

Committee members should be satisfied that they understand the interplay of all compensation arrangements—fixed, incentive, benefits, perquisites, deferred compensation, and severance—so that unintended or disproportionate benefits do not accrue to the senior executive. To facilitate this understanding, senior management at many public corporations annually provide committee members

> *Committee members should be satisfied that they understand the interplay of all compensation arrangements—fixed, incentive, benefits, perquisites, deferred compensation, and severance—so that unintended or disproportionate benefits do not accrue to the senior executive.*

with tally sheets containing a clear and comprehensive listing of all elements of compensation paid to each senior executive and the amount of each element, as well as the value of potential severance and change-in-control benefits to which the executive could become entitled. The need for an accurate computation of these amounts has been increased by the executive compensation disclosure rules adopted by the SEC in 2006. These rules require public corporations to disclose, with more detail than previously required, the dollar value of all elements of executive compensation, as well as estimates of benefits that could become payable to senior executives either upon a termination of employment or upon a change in control of the corporation.

The proper design of a compensation program is just the starting point. Application of the program requires at least annual performance evaluations of the participating executives against pre-established performance targets (which may include comparison against the performance of peer corporations), as well as ongoing review of the program's effectiveness. The committee should keep the board informed of the results of these periodic reviews.

3. *Documentation of Approval of Executive Compensation*

The compensation committee should review with senior management the corporation's procedures for accurately and timely documenting the grants of equity awards, both in the committee's minutes and in the documentation evidencing the awards. A corporation should have written procedures relating to the granting of equity awards, including the timing and pricing of grants, to help protect the corporation, its executives, and the committee against claims of manipulation or abuse in the timing or pricing of equity awards.

A corporation should have written procedures relating to the granting of equity awards, including the timing and pricing of grants, to help protect the corporation, its executives, and the committee against claims of manipulation or abuse in the timing or pricing of equity awards.

4. *Legal Restrictions on Executive Compensation*

The compensation committee should become familiar with and receive legal advice as to legal restrictions on compensation to officers and directors. Most personal loans and extensions or arrangements of credit from a public company to its directors and executive officers are prohibited. In addition, if the corporation is required to restate its financial statements due to misconduct, the CEO and CFO may be required to reimburse the corporation for any bonus or other incentive- or equity-based compensation received during the 12-month period following the first public issuance or filing with the SEC of the financial document that is subsequently restated. Any profits realized from the sale of securities of the corporation during this 12-month period may also have to be paid to the corporation. Also, the terms of any shareholder-approved plans may contain limitations that the committee has to follow.

Regardless of the requirements of the federal securities laws, in circumstances in which there has been a restatement indicating that the bases on which incentive-based compensation has been paid are no longer correct, the compensation committee or other independent directors should consider whether action should be taken to recover any such compensation on the basis of unjust enrichment. In addition, if the restatement has resulted from misconduct, the committee or other independent directors should consider whether action should be taken to discipline or dismiss, as well as to recover compensation paid to, any employee involved in the misconduct.

C. Disclosure of Compensation Decisions

Public company managers are required to prepare a section of the annual meeting proxy statement called Compensation Discussion and Analysis, which is a detailed discussion of the key elements of executive compensation policies and decisions. This disclosure is focused on the principles underlying executive compensation decisions. The Compensation Discussion and Analysis must include a discussion of the following:

- the objectives of the corporation's compensation programs;
- what the compensation program is designed to reward;
- each element of compensation;

- why the corporation chooses to pay each element;
- how the corporation determines the amount (and the formula, if any) for each element of pay; and
- how each compensation element and the corporation's decisions regarding that element fit into the corporation's overall compensation objectives and affect decisions regarding other compensation elements.

Because many of the compensation decisions for senior executives will be made outside the presence of management, the committee should assist management in its preparation of the Compensation Discussion and Analysis and then review and be satisfied with it. In addition, the committee's separate report in the proxy statement must state that the members of the committee have reviewed and discussed the Compensation Discussion and Analysis with management and, based on this review and discussion, recommended that it be included in the proxy statement.

The compensation committee should scrutinize closely the corporation's policies and procedures relating to the disclosure of executive officer and director compensation. The committee should seek appropriate assurances from management and legal counsel that all disclosures required by law and by the applicable securities market listing standards are being made, and that rules related to shareholder approval of stock option plans and the reporting of trades in the corporation's securities are being observed. The compensation committee, along with counsel, should consider how to document adequately the process supporting the disclosures.

D. Independent Advice for the Committee

The compensation committee should be empowered to hire (without management influence in the selection process) outside counsel, compensation specialists, consulting firms, or other experts to assist in the evaluation of director, CEO, and senior executive compensation so that it need not rely solely upon corporate personnel or outside specialists selected by management for advice and guidance. The committee's need for independent advice is particularly critical when the committee exercises its obligations with respect to reviewing and approving employment agreements with executives. The compensation committee should have full authority, stated in its charter, to approve its advisor's fees and other terms of engagement and should make clear that the advisor works for the compensation committee, not management. The advisor should have direct access to the compensation committee without the presence of the CEO or other senior executives to help preserve the advisor's independence. Outside advisors should also have direct access to senior executives in order to obtain information necessary to provide the compensation committee independent advice.

The committee should be aware of the selection process for its own compensation specialists or consulting firm and should participate in that process. The committee should also be kept aware of any relationships between such compensation specialists or consultants and the corporation.

E. Other Responsibilities

Other responsibilities that the compensation committee may undertake include reviewing and monitoring the effectiveness of employee pension, profit sharing, 401(k), and other benefit plans, taking into account the importance of retaining and motivating the employees of the corporation, as well as the overall cost to the corporation of such programs. Compensation committees should carefully consider whether they are or should be fiduciaries with respect to the corporation's pension, 401(k), or other employee benefits plans that are subject to regulation under the Employee Retirement Income Security Act (ERISA). Under ERISA, plan fiduciaries are subject to heightened scrutiny and responsibility with respect to the investment of plan assets. The compensation committee has a duty to be informed about the corporation's compensation and benefit structure; however, most compensation committees do not act as the fiduciary for ERISA-covered benefit plans. Directors and high-level executives typically are privy to nonpublic information regarding the corporation's performance and finances, which can place them in the difficult position of having to choose between their duties as officers or directors under state and federal laws to keep such information confidential and their duties as plan fiduciaries possibly to disclose or act upon such information for the benefit of plan participants. Often, rather than having directors or senior officers designated as plan fiduciaries, corporation employees (but not the most senior executives) will serve as the fiduciaries of the corporation's ERISA plans. Increasingly, however, corporations are engaging independent fiduciaries to make some or all of the investment decisions for their ERISA-covered plans in order to insulate the corporation from potential conflicts of interest related to such investment decisions, particularly with respect to any decisions to invest plan assets in the stock of the corporation.

Nominating/Corporate Governance Committee

The independence and quality of director nominees are critical to creating a board with a majority of independent directors and enhancing the effective functioning of the board. The recruitment and selection of new independent directors and the evaluation of incumbent directors are functions of a nominating committee. An increasing number of public companies have transformed the board's "nominating committee" into the "corporate governance committee" or the "nominating/corporate governance committee." The change in name reflects the committee's expanded role to address corporate governance principles and practices, in addition to selecting director nominees and making committee assignments. Some functions of a nominating/corporate governance committee are prescribed by the major securities markets' listing standards. Smaller public companies may prefer to combine these functions with those of other committees of independent directors, such as the compensation committee.

A. Committee Composition and Other Requirements

The nominating/corporate governance committee should be composed solely of independent directors. In general, absent special circumstances, the NASDAQ Stock Market requires that director nominations be approved either by independent directors acting as an independent nominating/corporate governance committee or by a majority of the independent directors acting in executive session. The NYSE requires that each of its listed companies have a committee composed entirely of independent directors, with a written charter that addresses the committee's purpose to identify individuals qualified to become directors, to select, or to recommend that the board select, director nominees, and to develop and recommend to the board a set of corporate governance principles for the corporation.

B. Criteria for Board Membership

One of the most important functions of the nominating/corporate governance committee is to establish, or recommend to the board, criteria for identifying appropriate director candidates. The principal attributes of an effective corporate director include strength of character, an inquiring and independent mind, practical wisdom, and mature judgment. In addition to these personal qualities, the committee may want to establish individual qualifications such as technical skills, career specialization, or specific industry or other relevant experience. Specific talents and special areas of substantive expertise are qualities that should be evaluated when considering whether to nominate individuals for service on a board of directors. Corporations can greatly benefit from directors with diverse and relevant areas of expertise and experience. Indeed, SEC regulations require that a corporation identify a director who qualifies as an "audit committee financial expert" for accounting and financial reporting purposes, or explain why it does not have such an expert. In recent years, public companies have added diversity considerations to their desired board profile, recognizing that diversity can contribute significant value in providing additional perspectives to board deliberations. The articles of incorporation, bylaws, or board policies may include other qualifications for directors, such as age or length of service limitations or relevant experience.

In mounting a search for a new director, many committees construct a profile of skills and experiences that the board currently possesses, lacks, or needs to strengthen. Focusing on the board's strengths and weaknesses has proven helpful in directing the search toward candidates who can provide needed additional talent and experience to the corporation. The nominating committee should have the discretion to consider the qualifications and attributes that are best suited to the corporation's specific circumstances.

Most corporate governance commentators recommend that a board of a public company consist of a substantial majority of independent directors, and the major securities markets require at least a majority of independent directors, as defined by each market. When addressing a director's independence, the committee should also bear in mind the broader judicial standard of disinterestedness that will be applied when conflict of interest matters are reviewed in court, and should therefore consider the full range of business and personal relationships between director candidates and the corporation and its senior managers.

Although the securities markets require a majority of the directors to be independent, the board must be able to receive candid input from senior management. The committee should consider how best to receive this input and have access to senior management. Some nominating/corporate governance committees determine that senior officers other than the CEO should also serve as directors, whereas others decide that attendance at board meetings by senior officers in a non-director capacity is sufficient to facilitate the board's ready access to information regarding the business and operations of the corporation. It is not unusual for the committee to select one or two board positions for senior executives (in addition to the CEO) in order to evaluate their succession prospects and to facilitate a peer relationship and firsthand contact with them.

Boards should consider the desirability of term limits or a mandatory retirement age for directors to enable the board to gain fresh perspectives from new board members from time to time. A well-functioning nominating committee should be able to decline to nominate incumbents for reelection as individual situations dictate, without any such limits or requirements.

C. Nominating Directors

The nominating/corporate governance committee approves and selects, or recommends that the board select, director nominees, including both incumbent directors and new candidates. The committee also recommends candidates to be elected by the board to fill an interim director vacancy.

Typically, the nominating process entails periodic review by the committee of the performance and the contributions of current directors as well as the need for and qualifications of prospective directors. This review is a key element of good corporate governance because the board is likely to adopt the committee's recommendations and, unless a contest is mounted, the majority of the shareholders' votes cast are likely to support the nominees recommended by the board.

All directors, including management directors, should be encouraged to suggest candidates for the board, but the committee should have a leading role in the final determination. There is a growing interest in having the nominating/corporate governance committee be more responsive to shareholder recommendations for director nominees, and it may be prudent for a

There is a growing interest in having the nominating/corporate governance committee be more responsive to shareholder recommendations for director nominees, and it may be prudent for a committee to consider suggestions from its institutional investors and other shareholders.

committee to consider suggestions from its institutional investors and other shareholders. The committee's charter should give the committee the authority to retain a search firm to identify director candidates, including the authority to approve the search firm's fees and other retention terms. The non-executive chair, if there is one, as well as the lead or presiding director or nominating/corporate governance committee chair, should be prominently involved in the recruiting process in order to reinforce the perception as well as the reality that the nominating decisions are being made by the committee and not by the CEO or other insiders.

One criticism often directed against corporate boards is that initial election (often by the board to fill a vacancy) is tantamount to an award of tenure. A thoughtful review by the committee of a director's contribution and the needs of the board, before deciding whether to recommend renomination, is the most effective mechanism to address this criticism. The committee should evaluate each director who is approaching the end of his or her term in light of that individual's participation and contributions, as well as the standards or criteria that have been developed for board membership and the needs of the board for certain types of background, experience, and expertise. It is the committee's responsibility to determine, in each case, whether renomination of a director is appropriate generally and in light of any bylaw restrictions. The committee may find it helpful to seek the views of the other directors. Given the interpersonal relationships involved, this review should be conducted in a fair and discreet manner.

Public companies must disclose in their proxy statements the procedures and policies followed by the nominating/corporate governance committee in considering director candidates. These disclosure requirements are intended to enhance shareholder understanding of the nominating process. Accordingly, the nominating/corporate governance committee should review its procedures and policies to ensure that they fit the committee's circumstances and operations and that they are sufficiently formalized to satisfy the scrutiny of public disclosure. In addition, the SEC continues to consider the circumstances or conditions under which shareholders should be able to include their director nominees in the corporation's proxy statement. In July 2007, the SEC proposed to allow more than 5% shareholders to include, in the corporation's proxy statement, bylaw proposals to create company-specific nomination procedures whereby, if the proposed bylaw amendments were approved, shareholders could include their director nominees in the corporation's proxy statement.

D. Recommending Committee Members and Chairs

In addition to nominating directors, the nominating/corporate governance committee will often make recommendations to the board regarding the responsibilities, organization, and membership of all board committees. The committee should recommend to the board the responsibilities and functions of board committees, together with the qualifications for membership on each committee. Consideration should be given to a policy of periodic rotation among the directors of committee memberships and the responsibilities of chairing committees. Because of the skills and background experience required for audit committee members, a policy of rotation may be more difficult to implement for members of that committee than for members of other committees. The nominating/corporate governance committee should also address the process for the committee's recommendations to the board for the appointment of and changes in the chair and members of each board committee.

E. Chief Executive Officer and Other Management Succession

One of the most important decisions that a board makes is selecting a new CEO and providing for succession plans so that the corporation does not suffer due to a vacancy in leadership, especially an unexpected one. The CEO will hire the other members of the senior management team and implement the corporation's strategic direction with input and guidance from the board. The CEO will establish in large part the "tone at the top" for the corporation regarding compliance with laws and ethical standards generally. The CEO will also be directly responsible for the short- and long-term performance of the corporation, under the oversight of the board of directors.

> *One of the most important decisions that a board makes is selecting a new CEO and providing for succession plans so that the corporation does not suffer due to a vacancy in leadership, especially an unexpected one.*

Consequently, the board must select the CEO with care and due consideration for the challenges facing the corporation. Equally important, the board is responsible for monitoring the CEO's performance over time and must determine whether there is a need for a change in senior management, including the CEO, in light of the CEO's performance and the corporation's challenges.

A board facing the decision whether to retain or terminate the employment of a CEO must consider the best interests of the corporation, weighing the CEO's strengths and weaknesses against the challenges facing the corporation. These discussions may take place in executive sessions of the board or in committee meetings. If a change is deemed necessary, the board must consider immediate leadership transition issues, the possible need for and initiation of a search process for a replacement beyond the interim period, the need for communications to a variety of constituencies regarding the decision, and other management succession issues.

The nominating/corporate governance committee will often have the responsibility to recommend to the board a selection process or a successor to the CEO in the event of retirement or termination of service. The committee may also review and approve proposed changes in other senior management positions, with the understanding that the CEO should be given considerable discretion in selecting and retaining members of the management team. In order to perform these functions, the committee should—to the extent not done by another board committee—at least annually review the performance of the CEO and members of senior management. It should also periodically update succession planning and related procedures, including emergency procedures for management succession in the event of the unexpected death, disability, or departure of the CEO, and should review with the CEO management's plans for the replacement of other members of the senior management team.

F. Other Corporate Governance Functions

In addition to addressing director nomination or renomination, committee membership, and management evaluation and succession, the nominating/corporate governance committee typically addresses some or all of the following tasks and issues:

- developing, recommending to the board, and monitoring a statement of corporate governance principles or guidelines (required of listed companies by the major securities markets);
- evaluating the effectiveness of the board and board committees (also required of listed companies);
- evaluating the effectiveness of senior management (also required of listed companies);
- providing for director education programs;
- reviewing the board committee structure, including each committee's charter and size and the possible addition of other committees, such as finance or public policy committees;
- reviewing and making recommendations with respect to the corporation's director policies, such as compensation, retirement, indemnification, and insurance; and
- examining board meeting policies, such as meeting schedule and location, meeting agenda, the presence and participation of non-director senior executives, and written materials distributed in advance of meetings.

G. Director Compensation

The nominating/corporate governance committee should periodically consider the form and amount of director compensation. In doing so, it often works in conjunction with the compensation committee. Directors have an unavoidable conflict of interest in fixing their own compensation. This problem is not ameliorated if director compensation programs are suggested by management or by a compensation consultant. Recognizing that they have the responsibility to determine their own compensation, directors normally make sure they have the information necessary to reach a fair decision, including data on peer companies, together with an analysis of any special factors that may relate to their particular corporation, such as the expected time commitment.

Director compensation programs should be designed to closely align the directors' interests with the long-term interests of the corporation. Director compensation may take a number of different forms, including annual stock or cash retainers, attendance fees for board and committee meetings, deferred compensation plans, stock options, and restricted stock grants. Additional compensation is also sometimes paid for serving as a committee chair or as a member of a standing committee. The corporation's executives generally do not receive additional compensation for serving on the board.

SEC rules require detailed disclosure of all elements of director compensation, including perquisites and charitable donation programs. Values should be estimated, and taken into account, for any non-monetary items such as stock options or restricted stock grants. Any consulting or other agreements with directors and any material payments to directors for consulting or other services beyond the regular directors' fees should be carefully considered, as they may impair independence, and in any event must be disclosed to shareholders in the annual proxy statement.

The board should be sensitive to and avoid compensation policies or corporate perquisites that might impair the independence of its non-management directors. To maintain directors' focus on proper long-range corporate objectives, most corporations now pay some component of compensation in the form of stock options and/or restricted stock grants on the the-

The board should be sensitive to and avoid compensation policies or corporate perquisites that might impair the independence of its non-management directors.

ory that these forms of equity compensation strengthen the directors' interest in the overall success of the corporation and better align their personal interests with those of shareholders. Because options alone do not involve acceptance of any economic risk by a director, some companies require directors to purchase a minimum amount of stock in the open market or to accept at least a designated portion of their compensation in stock grants rather than cash. In addition, some companies have instituted policies requiring directors to hold for a minimum period shares resulting from the exercise of stock options (less sales necessary to fund option exercise and pay commissions and taxes). Directors' retirement arrangements, insurance policies, and educational or charitable gift programs— once somewhat widespread—have been criticized by some shareholder groups as not being related to corporate performance. As a result, they have generally been reduced or discontinued as forms of director compensation.

Corporate Governance and the Election Process

A. Corporate Governance

Corporate governance is an important aspect of directors' responsibilities. The board's responsibility to oversee the management of the business and affairs of the corporation includes striking the right balance between the interests and concerns of shareholders (the composition of which is often a fluid mix of unaffiliated investors) and those of senior management, which is responsible for running the day-to-day operations of the corporation. Shareholders elect directors, but do not run the corporation. At the same time, shareholders often advance legitimate concerns about the corporation or its performance.

Corporate governance encompasses a wide variety of issues affecting the corporation and its shareholders, including the composition and experience of the board, committee structure and composition, executive compensation, succession planning, the structure of the director election process (e.g., majority voting), charter or bylaw provisions (e.g., staggered board provisions), and the relationship of the board to senior executives (including proposals to split the positions of board chair and CEO). Boards may want to develop legal or business strategies to address these issues on their own initiative before being pressured to do so by shareholders. Boards may also want to develop their own communication policies or practices with shareholders, as shareholder groups are increasingly requesting an audience with the independent directors or with an independent board committee to discuss their issues and concerns.

The board should address corporate governance seriously. There is an important difference between corporate governance initiatives that interfere with the corporation's established strategies and objectives and those that advance legitimate concerns. The board's challenge is balancing the many, sometimes conflicting, interests in overseeing the corporation for the benefit of all shareholders.

> *There is an important difference between corporate governance initiatives that interfere with the corporation's established strategies and objectives and those that advance legitimate concerns. The board's challenge is balancing the many, sometimes conflicting, interests in overseeing the corporation for the benefit of all shareholders.*

B. Election Process

The directors of a corporation are elected by the shareholders of the corporation and have a duty to advance the interests of the corporation to the exclusion of their own interests. They are accountable to the corporation's shareholders who, if dissatisfied with the directors' performance, can, depending on state law and the articles of incorporation and bylaws, decline to reelect them or, in many cases where the articles and bylaws allow, remove them from office even before their terms are over.

Directors generally are elected to serve for a one-year term or, if a corporation's articles of incorporation provide for a classified or "staggered" board, for a longer term. Typically, directors on a classified board will serve for staggered three-year terms. The principal benefit of a classified board is to ensure continuity of leadership. In recent years, shareholder activists have criticized classified boards as they can also operate as a takeover defense. This is because it is difficult for shareholders to unseat directors in the period between elections, when directors on a classified board may be removed (under some state statutes) only for cause. As with most aspects of corporate governance, there is no single answer as to whether a classified board is appropriate in a particular circumstance.

Traditionally, directors are elected by a plurality vote, which means that the candidates with the highest number of votes in their favor are elected, up to the maximum number of directorships available. This standard ensures a successful election. For that reason, the plurality standard has generally been considered preferable to a requirement that a candidate receive a majority (or some other fixed portion) of the votes cast. Significant negative consequences can flow from an election that does not result in the valid election of the requisite number of (or any) duly elected directors. State laws generally seek to avoid a situation when a company has no directors by providing that incumbent directors "hold over" as directors until their successors are elected.

Historically, the vast majority of elections for corporate directors have not been contested. A slate of directors is chosen and nominated by the incumbent directors (in many cases on recommendation by a nominating committee of the board), who recommend that the shareholders vote for that slate. Although shareholders generally have the right to nominate their own candidates if they are not satisfied with the board's nominees, the solicitation of proxies from other shareholders is necessary in order for their candidates to have any chance of being elected, and this solicitation must comply with the SEC's proxy solicitation rules. Because this can be a relatively expensive and time-consuming process, it is not lightly—or very often—undertaken. (An exception is in the case of a takeover attempt when the high stakes justify the effort and expense.)

In recent years, shareholder activists have been using "withhold the vote" campaigns to signal their disapproval of board candidates, instead of proposing alternative nominees. Although this does not affect the legal outcome of the election in a plurality vote system in which there are no competing candidates, there have been some prominent instances in which a large percentage of "withheld" votes from one or more candidates have been followed by a change in the board. This demonstrates that "withhold the vote" campaigns can be powerful catalysts for change. More often, however, withholding one's vote is largely a symbolic way for a shareholder to register disapproval.

Although plurality voting remains the standard by which most directors are elected today, many boards have adopted a majority voting standard. There are numerous possible formulations of majority voting, but in general, the majority voting standard requires a candidate to garner more votes cast in favor than against (or withheld) in order to be elected and to serve as a director.

> *Although plurality voting remains the standard by which most directors are elected today, many boards have adopted a majority voting standard.*

Some companies have adopted majority voting as their default election standard. Many more have adopted either bylaws or board policies retaining plurality voting as the underlying standard for election but requiring candidates who fail to receive a majority of the vote to tender their resignation to the board. In most cases, an exception is included for contested elections, where plurality voting continues to apply.

A full discussion of this complex subject is beyond the scope of this *Guidebook*, but it is very likely that over the next few years, majority voting (in its many forms) will become more prevalent among public companies.

Duties Under the Federal Securities Laws

Federal and state laws regulate the disclosure practices and securities transactions of public companies and their directors, officers, and employees. The federal securities laws are administered by the SEC and affect many daily activities of public companies. Violation of these laws can result in significant civil and criminal penalties, imposed not only on the corporation but also potentially on individual directors. Directors need to be particularly attentive to their own, as well as the corporation's, compliance with these laws. Review of programs and policies designed to maintain compliance with the federal securities laws, absent assignment of responsibilities to a legal compliance committee, is often delegated to the audit committee.

A corporation must maintain effective systems of internal financial and disclosure controls and procedures for collecting, reviewing, and disclosing financial and other material information about the corporation. Quarterly review and certification of the effectiveness of systems and procedures that support SEC filings are required of the CEO and the CFO of public companies. Annual evaluation of internal control over financial reporting by management and the audit of internal control over financial reporting by the external auditor are also required for many companies and scheduled to become required for others. The board, generally through its audit committee, should receive and examine reports concerning each of these reviews.

A. SEC Reporting Requirements

Public companies must file both periodic and current reports with the SEC. Periodic reports include an annual report on Form 10-K and quarterly reports on Form 10-Q, both of which require the disclosure of specified financial and other information. Current reports on Form 8-K are required for disclosure of quarterly earnings releases, material contracts, changes in management, director resignations, and a broad spectrum of other specified events. A Form 8-K may also be used for voluntary disclosure of information. The SEC's proxy rules require that the annual meeting proxy statement be accompanied or preceded by an annual report to shareholders.

The corporation's annual report on Form 10-K contains the last fiscal year's audited financial statements, as well as management's discussion and analysis of the corporation's results of operation and financial condition and important trends and uncertainties. The Form 10-K is the most detailed of the reports filed with the SEC, and it must be signed by a majority of the corporation's directors. Separate and apart from the audit committee's involvement, all directors should review and be satisfied with the corporate processes used to prepare the Form 10-K and understand the significant disclosures in that report. Therefore, the full board should have an opportunity to read, comment on, and ask questions about the Form 10-K before it is filed.

Directors are not expected to verify independently the accuracy of underlying facts contained in earnings releases or reports filed with the SEC, but they should be satisfied that the disclosures are not contrary to the facts as they know them. In addition, the audit committee and the board should be satisfied that there are disclosure controls and procedures in place reasonably designed to achieve the timeliness, accuracy, and completeness of annual and quarterly reports as well as all other reports and public releases. In addition, the CEO and CFO of public companies are required to review and, based on their knowledge, certify the material accuracy and completeness of quarterly and annual reports. Quarterly assessments of disclosure controls and procedures and annual assessments of internal control over financial reporting are also required. Audit committee members of public companies should be familiar with these certifications and assessments and the procedures undertaken to support them, and the audit committee should always be attentive to reports of control deficiencies, especially material weaknesses.

B. Registration Statements

Directors should take diligent steps to assure the accuracy of their corporation's registration statements filed with the SEC in connection with any offering (including in a merger or acquisition) of the corporation's securities to the public. Regardless of whether a director actually signs the registration statement, the director may be liable for any material inaccuracy or omission in the registration statement, including information incorporated by reference from other filed documents, unless the director establishes that, after due diligence, the director was not aware of the inaccuracy or omission.

> *Regardless of whether a director actually signs the registration statement, the director may be liable for any material inaccuracy or omission in the registration statement, including information incorporated by reference from other filed documents, unless the director establishes that, after due diligence, the director was not aware of the inaccuracy or omission.*

The director's primary defense to registration statement liability is due diligence. To establish this defense, the director must show that, after reasonable investigation, the director had reasonable grounds to believe and did believe that the registration statement did not contain any materially false or misleading statements or any material omissions that made the registration statement misleading. Actions required by the director to satisfy the due diligence standard will vary with the circumstances. During the registration process, directors are well advised to satisfy themselves that the corporation has developed and uses appropriate corporate disclosure controls and procedures reasonably designed to ensure the registration statement's accuracy and completeness. Although all registration statements should be prepared with appropriate care, certain registered offerings may have a higher potential for liability, such as an initial public offering, a follow-on equity offering, or a financing or reorganization of a public company that has experienced problems. Accordingly, a board meeting or meetings with counsel, accountants, and management present at which there is discussion and analysis of the disclosures in the registration statement should precede the filing of registration statements for such offerings.

Each director should personally review the registration statement for accuracy, with particular attention to those statements and disclosures in the registration statement that are within the director's knowledge and competence. Directors may also want to consider consulting with the corporation's legal counsel to understand any material changes made to disclosure documents in response to SEC comments and to confirm specifically that the process followed fulfills the due diligence requirements.

For many companies, the disclosures found in the company's Form 10-K and other reports filed previously with the SEC are incorporated into the registration statement. Therefore, the procedures that were followed to review these reports are important when there is a registered securities offering.

C. Insider Trading

The federal securities laws prohibit corporate insiders, including directors, and the corporation itself from purchasing or selling the corporation's securities, either in the open market or in private transactions, when they possess material, nonpublic information about the corporation. The corporation or an insider in possession of such information may not take actions involving the securities until the information is publicly disseminated. Policies should be adopted to address securities transactions, including transactions in 401(k) plans and gifts of securities. The federal securities laws also prohibit insiders from revealing material, nonpublic information concerning the corporation, or giving a recommendation to buy or sell based upon such information, to others who trade based upon such information. As a general rule, the federal securities laws also prohibit the recipient of a tip from acting on material, nonpublic information obtained from a corporate source. Under the SEC's Rule 10b5-1, directors and other insiders can mitigate the risk of insider trading liability by adopting plans in advance for scheduled sales and purchases of the corporation's securities.

Information is material if there is a substantial likelihood that a reasonable investor would consider it important in deciding whether to buy, sell, or hold a security. Some believe that information may be considered material if, upon disclosure, it would likely affect the stock price. If there is any doubt whether undisclosed information is material, legal guidance should be sought or, as a practical alternative, the information should be treated as material.

Violation of any of these insider trading laws triggers strict sanctions. The violator is liable for any profit made or loss avoided. In addition, a court can assess a penalty against the trader, the tipper, or the tippee of treble damages—that is, three times the profits made or losses avoided. Criminal sanctions are also possible.

The SEC has an aggressive program of discovering and proceeding against insider trading violations. The SEC can award informants who report a violation up to 10% of the amount of the penalty recovered. The SEC also can prohibit any individual from serving as an officer or director of any public company if the individual has violated the antifraud or insider trading laws and demonstrates unfitness to serve as an officer or director. In addition to potential violations of federal law, the misuse of confidential corporate information can result in violations of directors' duties under state law, leading to civil lawsuits brought by shareholders.

Many public companies have procedures requiring senior executives and directors to contact corporate counsel, the corporate secretary, or another designated person before any trading in the corporation's securities so that any proposed transaction can be reviewed in the light of the current state of public information. Many public companies have policies prohibiting insiders and their affiliates from trading in the corporation's securities during specified "blackout" periods. The board of directors (directly or through its audit or legal compliance committee) should periodically review corporate information disclosure and insider trading policies and procedures in view of Regulation FD (discussed below) and insider trading prohibitions.

D. Reporting Share Ownership and Transactions; Short-Swing Profits

Directors, executive officers, and more than 10% shareholders of public companies must report to the SEC all their holdings of and transactions in the corporation's equity securities and must disgorge to the corporation any profits realized from buying and selling (or selling and buying) such securities within any six-month period. When a person first becomes an insider (i.e., a director, executive officer, or more than 10% shareholder), a report of beneficial ownership of the corporation's equity securities must be filed and thereafter whenever there is a change in beneficial ownership. These reports must be filed on a timely basis—two business days for changes in beneficial ownership. All delinquent filings must be disclosed in the corporation's annual meeting proxy statement (with the delinquent individuals identified by name), and they can trigger monetary fines. An insider is generally deemed to be the owner of securities that are owned by a spouse or child living with the insider, and may also be deemed to be the owner of securities held in a trust of which the insider is a trustee, settlor, or beneficiary or of securities owned by a corporation or other entity controlled by the insider.

> *Directors, executive officers, and more than 10% shareholders of public companies must report to the SEC all their holdings of and transactions in the corporation's equity securities and must disgorge to the corporation any profits realized from buying and selling (or selling and buying) such securities within any six-month period.*

Profit disgorgement is required if an insider purchases and sells the corporation's securities within a six-month period and vice versa (i.e., sells within six months before buying). Any "profit"—measured as the difference between the prices of any two "matchable" transactions during the six-month period (i.e., the highest priced sale and the lowest priced purchase)—must be paid to the corporation. The requirement is intentionally arbitrary and, subject to tightly defined regulatory exemptions, applies to all transactions within any six-month period regardless of whether the insider had inside information or, in fact, made a profit on an overall basis. This provision is aggressively enforced by a plaintiffs' bar that monitors SEC filings.

Some transactions, such as the grant and exercise of stock options and the acquisition of securities under employee benefit plans, may be exempt from the purchase and sale triggers of the short-swing profit rules if procedural requirements established by SEC rules have been satisfied. Absent an exemption, the receipt of an option, the acquisition of securities through a benefit plan, or the acquisition of a derivative security related to the value of the corporation's common stock normally will be considered to be a purchase of the underlying security and could be matchable against a sale. Unexpected liability may result from the application of the short-swing profit rules. For example, other indirect changes in ownership, such as intracompany transactions, pledges, and mergers, may be considered a purchase or sale transaction for purposes of the short-swing profit rules.

A retiring director may be subject to profit recovery based on transactions occurring during the six months after the director departs. If a director purchases shares of the corporation, resigns, and sells shares within six months after the purchase, liability may be imposed for any short-swing profit even though the individual is no longer a director at the time of the sale.

Directors, officers, and more than 10% shareholders also are prohibited from selling the corporation's shares short; as a means to enforce this restriction, they are required to deliver shares against a sale within 20 days.

This regulatory regime is highly technical. Legal counsel should be consulted before committing to a transaction in the corporation's securities or in options or other derivatives geared to its securities.

E. Sales by Controlling Persons

Unless an exemption is available, the federal securities laws generally require registration with the SEC of the corporation's securities before those securities can be offered or sold to the public by "controlling persons." (Determining who is a controlling person is a complex question of law and fact for which legal guidance is advisable; directors are often considered to be "controlling persons.") The most common exemption is provided by the SEC's Rule 144, which permits the sale of limited amounts of securities without registration if certain conditions are satisfied. Securities acquired by a controlling person in the open market or in a registered offering are subject to the conditions in this rule, which include special filing and disclosure requirements, if they are to be sold to the public.

F. Proxy Statements

Public companies soliciting proxies for shareholder votes on the election of directors or other matters must furnish each shareholder a proxy statement. If actions other than election of directors or other routine business are to be taken, a preliminary proxy statement must be filed with, and often will be reviewed and cleared by, the SEC. In other cases, only the final proxy statement, as distributed, is filed with the SEC. Directors should be attentive to the procedures followed in preparing the corporation's proxy statements. It is good practice for every director to review a reasonably close-to-final draft of the proxy statement before it is distributed or filed with the SEC, particularly sections dealing with matters about which the director has personal knowledge (such as any related person transaction involving the director) or containing a report of a committee on which the director serves. Similar disclosure requirements can apply when corporate action is being taken without soliciting proxies.

The proxy statement for the annual shareholder meeting must include information about the company's directors, officers, and principal shareholders, as well as about certain of its governance policies. It must also include extensive information about the company's compensation of its officers and directors, both in tabular and narrative form, including a detailed discussion of the company's compensation objectives, policies, and practices.

G. Fair Disclosure

The SEC's Regulation FD (for "fair disclosure") provides that material information about a public company may not be disclosed on a selective basis by the corporation or its agents to marketplace participants, such as analysts, brokers, investment advisors, and shareholders who may act on the information and have not agreed to keep the information confidential. Rather, the corporation must take steps to disseminate such information in a manner that makes it broadly available to all market participants simultaneously. As a result, directors should be careful not to disclose nonpublic information about the corporation and its business. Violations of Regulation FD have resulted in SEC enforcement actions and fines against public companies and corporate officers. Regulation FD has caused public companies to adopt more restrictive policies regarding the persons who are authorized to speak on behalf of the company with securities analysts and others. It has also prompted many companies to make more information public.

H. Compliance Programs

Many public companies have established specific policies and procedures dealing with public communications, share ownership reporting, and insider trading. These programs are designed to ensure that the corporation makes complete, accurate, and timely disclosure of material information, complies with the registration requirements, and satisfies other securities law obligations. These programs also help directors and other insiders to comply with insider trading and other applicable laws and the corporation to meet its obligations under Regulation FD to avoid improper selective disclosure of material information. The audit committee (or the legal compliance committee, if there is one) generally should monitor the establishment and operation of such compliance programs.

I. Directors of Non-U.S. Corporations with Securities Traded in the United States

A large number of non-U.S. corporations file reports with the SEC because their securities are traded on U.S. securities markets or they have a large number of U.S. holders. Traditionally, the federal securities laws have required these "foreign private issuers" to file annual reports and other material information distributed to their shareholders with the SEC but have not otherwise sought to regulate their corporate governance and other internal practices.

The Sarbanes-Oxley Act's reporting and corporate governance requirements generally apply to non-U.S. corporations that have securities registered with the SEC. The SEC, in adopting rules under the Sarbanes-Oxley Act, has considered the concerns of foreign private issuers and made some rules inapplicable to them or included special provisions addressing their concerns. Directors of foreign private issuers should be aware of the general categories of substantive corporate governance requirements that may apply to their corporations.

Liabilities, Indemnification, and Insurance

Directors may incur personal liability for breaches of their duty of care or their duty of loyalty or for failure to satisfy regulatory legal requirements, such as the federal securities laws. It is common for corporations to provide directors (and officers) appropriate indemnification rights and insurance, and directors may want to ensure that appropriate expertise is involved in handling these complex matters.

> *It is common for corporations to provide directors (and officers) appropriate indemnification rights and insurance, and directors may want to ensure that appropriate expertise is involved in handling these complex matters.*

A. State Law Liability

The laws of most states generally provide that directors will have met their duty of care to the corporation if they discharge their responsibilities (i) with an informed judgment, (ii) with a measure of care that a person in a like position would reasonably believe appropriate under similar circumstances, and (iii) in a manner they reasonably believe to be in the best interests of the corporation. Courts may impose liability against directors for gross negligence or an obvious or prolonged failure to participate diligently or to exercise oversight and supervision. Recent decisions of the Delaware Chancery and Supreme Courts, as well as increased public awareness of and sensitivity to corporate governance issues, underscore the need for directors to take an active role in meeting their duties of care and loyalty if liability is to be avoided.

In transactions in which a director has a conflicting personal interest, extra precautions must be taken to avoid improper self-dealing and to satisfy the applicable legal requirements. Most state corporate statutes prescribe procedures that may be followed to obtain approval, authorization, or ratification of interested director transactions. The scope of protection gained from following these statutory procedures varies from state to state.

In addition to liability for breach of duties, directors can also be liable for authorizing unlawful dividends or other distributions. The distributions that are unlawful and give rise to director liability vary from state to state. Generally, unlawful distributions are those causing or made during insolvency, those violating applicable laws, or those prohibited by the corporation's articles of incorporation.

B. Federal Securities Law Liability

As discussed in Section 10 of this publication, directors can be personally liable under the federal securities laws—in some cases even where they act in good faith. In certain circumstances, negligence, by itself, will be sufficient to establish liability. In other situations, liability may be imposed, subject only to due diligence or other defenses, without a finding of fault or intent to deceive.

C. Liability under Other Laws

Directors also can be subject to personal liability under other state and federal statutes, such as environmental laws. Good faith and careful monitoring of management programs directed toward corporate legal compliance should pro-vide substantial safeguards against any such personal liability.

D. Limitation of Liability

Most state corporation statutes permit a corporation's charter to include a provision eliminating or limiting the liability of directors to the corporation and its shareholders for money damages for breaches of certain duties. Such a provision will most frequently eliminate exposure to claims involving breach of the duty of care. For instance, many states permit, with shareholder approval, a provision in the articles of incorporation eliminating or limiting directors' personal liability for money damages, except with respect to liability for a violation of the duty of loyalty, the receipt of a financial benefit to which a director is not entitled, the intentional infliction of harm on the corporation, an unlawful distribution, or an intentional violation of law. Some state statutes have additional exceptions. Protection from liability generally applies only to monetary liabilities to the corporation and its shareholders and not to injunctive relief or to liabilities to third parties, and the exculpatory provisions may not be effective to protect a director from liabilities resulting from federal law violations.

E. Indemnification

Most state corporation statutes specify the circumstances in which the corporation is required or permitted to indemnify directors against liability and to pay related reasonable expenses incurred in defending claims arising in connection with their service as directors. Many state statutes provide that indemnification for reasonable expenses (including court costs and attorneys' fees) is mandatory if the director has been wholly successful in the defense of any action, on the merits or otherwise. Statutory indemnification is often not mandatory if the director is not wholly successful. This may not be true in the case of charter or contractual indemnification.

A standard for permissible indemnification in many states' statutes is that the individual director must have acted in good faith and with a reasonable belief that the director's conduct was in (or not opposed to) the best interests of the corporation. In the case of criminal proceedings, the director must also have had no reasonable cause to believe this conduct was unlawful. Such statutes give corporations the power to indemnify directors in actions by third parties, including class actions, for expenses (including attorneys' fees), judgments, fines, and amounts paid in settlement of the actions. In derivative actions brought in the name of the corporation itself, indemnification is allowed for expenses (including attorneys' fees), but if a director is found liable, indemnification is allowed only with court approval. Further, many statutes provide that amounts paid in settlement of a derivative action may be indemnified only if approved by a court. In the case of settlements or certain adverse court determinations in third-party actions, indemnification is permitted if authorized by the court or upon a determination by a majority of directors not involved in the action, by the shareholders, or by independent legal counsel that the director met the applicable standard of conduct.

Many corporations have charter or bylaw provisions requiring indemnification to the maximum extent legally permissible. Some corporations also have entered into indemnification contracts with their directors to provide mandatory indemnification to the fullest extent the applicable statute permits. The advantage of an indemnification contract is that it cannot be rescinded without the consent of the director, whereas a charter or bylaw provision may be subject to alteration or elimination by amendment, although typically the amendment will not be applied retroactively. Recent court decisions make it advisable for the corporation to be specifically obligated, by contract or bylaw provision, to reimburse directors for reasonable costs incurred in enforcing the indemnification to which they are entitled. Also, indemnification may not be available for liabilities resulting from certain federal law violations, such as violations of the federal securities laws, if the indemnification is deemed to be contrary to public policy.

F. Advancement of Expenses

Because of the high cost of litigation, a director should determine whether the corporation is obligated to advance a director's defense costs if the director is sued. Most state corporation statutes permit the corporation to advance funds to directors to pay or reimburse reasonable expenses incurred by them in defense of a matter in litigation before the final disposition of the proceedings and before final determination of their right to indemnification for those

Directors generally must provide the corporation with an undertaking to repay any funds advanced by the corporation if it is ultimately determined that they are not entitled to indemnification.

expenses. Directors generally must provide the corporation with an undertaking to repay any funds advanced by the corporation if it is ultimately determined that they are not entitled to indemnification. As a general rule, advances for expenses are discretionary and made on a case-by-case basis upon authorization of the board of directors unless, as is often the case, mandatory advances are required by the articles of incorporation, bylaws, or contract. Provisions mandating indemnification, without making reference to advances, may be construed judicially as not also mandating advances; thus, an intent to make advances mandatory should be clearly stated in the provisions for mandatory indemnification set forth in the articles of incorporation, bylaws, or contract.

G. Insurance

Most corporations purchase directors' and officers' liability insurance covering (i) the corporation for any payment of indemnification and advances for expenses and (ii) directors and officers, if the corporation is unwilling to pay indemnification or advancement obligations (perhaps because of a change in control) or is unable to pay such obligations (perhaps because of insolvency or because the claim is one where indemnification or advance is not permitted). The relevant statutes of most jurisdictions permit the corporation to pay the premiums for this insurance. Because of recent uncertainty regarding the ability of directors and officers to access policies that also cover the corporation, some corporations have been exploring alternatives for coverage (e.g., policies that cover only nonmanagement directors).

Certain areas of activity such as environmental, employee benefit, or antitrust matters are often excluded from coverage under a typical policy. Conditions in existence at the time application for the insurance is made also may be excepted from coverage. Directors' and officers' insurance generally excludes fraud and criminal penalties and fines and sometimes excludes punitive damages. Insurance policies often exclude coverage for the same type of conduct for which state corporation statutes prohibit indemnification.

Insurance coverage is not available in every case. Most policies are written on a "claims made" (as compared to an "occurrence") basis, covering only defined claims lodged against directors during a specified period. In addition, the terms of coverage under differing policies are very complex and can vary greatly from insurer to insurer. Moreover, insurance markets change rapidly, and insurers may assert numerous reservations or defenses when claims are made. Therefore, directors are well advised to engage experts, who can also provide knowledgeable insight respecting current market conditions.

Although the amount of coverage is relevant, directors should also focus on the process employed to obtain or renew the coverage. Directors should ascertain the level of expertise within the corporation of the person responsible for negotiating the coverage or, in the alternative, determine whether an outside expert, familiar with current market conditions and policy and claim issues, has been retained to assist in such undertaking. For example, directors should take care in completing policy applications and questionnaires. Also relevant is the reputation of the insurance provider for handling insurance claims. This consideration can be more important than premium pricing because quarrels with the insurance carrier as to whether coverage is available when litigation materializes are clearly an unwanted distraction. In sum, directors' and officers' insurance is one of the most sophisticated policy arenas, and directors should seek assurance that the corporation's coverage does in fact afford the best protection obtainable in the current marketplace.

Conclusion

As discussed throughout this *Guidebook*, the legal requirements and constituency expectations that public company directors must address have changed significantly in recent years. Despite these changes, the core values associated with the corporate director's role—informed judgment, general oversight, and dedication to the corporation's best interests—continue to be the touchstone for evaluating directors' conduct.

In that vein, we conclude with these basic points:

- A director must exercise independent judgment for the overall benefit of the corporation.
- To meet the duty of care, a director must be diligent and invest significant time and energy in monitoring management's conduct of the business and compliance with the corporation's operating and administrative procedures and should be satisfied that the proper procedures are in place.
- A director should be comfortable that the board is appropriately informed and has had the time to deliberate carefully before making decisions, unless the circumstances warrant otherwise.
- A director is entitled to rely on performance by others of properly delegated functions and on reports, opinions, information, and statements of the corporation's officers, legal counsel, accountants, employees, and committees of the board on which the director does not serve when, under the circumstances, it is reasonable to do so.

- The duty of loyalty requires that directors not use their corporate position for an unauthorized personal benefit, gain, or other advantage at the expense of the corporation and that they not disregard their director duties.
- Conflicts of interest (including corporate opportunities and a director's transactions with the corporation) are not inherently improper. The manner in which an interested director and the board deal with a conflict situation determines the propriety of the transaction and the director's conduct.
- A periodic review of indemnification, expense advance, and insurance protections for directors is advisable.
- This *Guidebook* should not be viewed as a substitute for legal consultation and advice.

Appendix

Online Resources on Corporate Governance

United States

American Bar Association, Section of Business Law
www.abanet.org/buslaw/home.html

    Committee on Corporate Governance
    www.abanet.org/dch/committee.cfm?com=CL260000

    Committee on Corporate Laws
    www.abanet.org/dch/committee.cfm?com=CL270000

    Committee on Federal Regulation of Securities
    www.abanet.org/dch/committee.cfm?com-CL410000

American Bar Association Task Force on Corporate Responsibility
www.abanet.org/buslaw/corporateresponsibility

American Corporate Counsel Association
www.acca.com/

Boardroom INSIDER
www.boardroominsider.com

The Business Roundtable
www.businessroundtable.org/

CATO Institute: Corporate Governance
www.cato.org/current/corporate-governance/index.html

The Conference Board
www.conference-board.org

Corporate Governance Network
www.corpgov.net

The Corporate Library
www.thecorporatelibrary.com

Council of Institutional Investors
www.cii.org/

Delaware Corporate Law Clearinghouse
www.corporate-law.widener.edu

Institutional Shareholder Services
www.issproxy.com/

NASDAQ Stock Market, Inc.
www.nasdaq.com/newsroom/default.stm

National Association of Corporate Directors
www.nacdonline.org/

New York Stock Exchange
www.nyse.com

Securities Information
www.secinfo.com

Society of Corporate Secretaries and Governance Professionals
www.governanceprofessionals.org/

U.S. Securities and Exchange Commission
www.sec/gov

International

Asian Corporate Governance Association
www.acga-asia.org/index.cfm

Berlin Center of Corporate Governance
www.bccg.tu-berlin.de

Corporate Governance Japan
www.rieti.go.jp/cgj/en/index.htm

The European Commission: Modernization of Company Law
and Enhancement of Corporate Governance
www.ec.europa.eu/internal-
market/company/modern/index_en.htm

European Corporate Governance Institute
www.ecgi.org

Global Corporate Governance Forum
www.gcgf.org

Institute for International Corporate Governance
and Accountability
www.128.164.132.19/iicga

Institute of Directors in Southern Africa
www.iodsa.co.za

International Corporate Governance Network
www.icgn.org

International Institute for Corporate Governance
www.yccg.som.yale.edu

Organization for Economic Cooperation and Development
www.oecd.org

Proxinvest (France)
www.proxinvest.com

United Kingdom Institute of Chartered Secretaries
and Administrators
www.icsa.org.uk

United Kingdom Institute of Directors
www.iod.co.uk

VIP—Association of Institutional Shareholders
www.vip-cg.com

World Bank Corporate Governance
www.rru.worldbank.org/themes/corporategovernance